Chinese Satire
Sources and Quotations

Compiled and Edited by Xiuwu R. Liu

HERMIT STUDIO

Oxford, Ohio
2024

Published by Hermit Studio
701 Western Drive
Oxford, OH 45056

Amended version

Published in the United States

The period of the *Annals* was the beginning of calamity and ruin, / The Warring States still more increased its bitter and poison. / Neither Qin nor Han were able to leap over and surpass them, / Rather, they even more added to their ill-will and ruthlessness. / How could they have taken account of the lives of the populace / When they only profited themselves and satisfied their selfish desires.

Right down to now, to this day, / Deceit has had a myriad faces. / The glib and the flatterers blaze hotter by the day, / The firm and the able disappear and perish. / Pile lickers have trains of quadrigae, / While those of austere countenance travel by foot. / Those bowing and bending become the famous and powerful, / Those petting and patting become the puissant and brutal. / When the lofty and haughty oppose current mores, / They at once bring about calamity and disaster. / Those who pell-mell chase after things, / Grow richer by the day and more prosperous by the month. / In the turmoil, all together are confused— / What's warm, what's cold? / Perverse fellows are illustrious and advance, / Upright gentlemen are obscure and concealed.

—Zhao Yi, "*Fù* Satirizing the Age, Detesting Iniquity"

I have discovered many inconsistencies in Chinese history—the conclusions about success and failure reached in the Annals are senseless, and the ethics taught by the sages do not tally up. There must be some secret to success that has not been revealed by the ancient annalists and sages. At first, I was unable to penetrate their mysteries—as I thought about the characters from the Three Kingdoms period I became spontaneously enlightened to their secret—the secret of the ancients' success is nothing more than their *thickened face* and *blackened heart*.

—Li Zongwu, "Thick Black Theory"

Contents

Wu Jingzi (Wu Ching-tzu 吴敬梓)

Preface

This resource was compiled for a course in Chinese satire at Miami University. Meanwhile, other readers interested in China or satire may also find it useful. The quotations were selected from my larger collection, *Deflating Human Beings: Sources and Quotations from Around the World*. That collection had ranged much more widely than China and satire, which means its coverage of Chinese satire, though extensive, remained limited. In fact, most of the Chinese sources in that collection didn't include all the satirical sayings, stanzas, or passages. (For famous satires such as *Rulin waishi* (The scholars) or *Wei cheng* (Fortress besieged), only a small number of quotes were selected.) Another limitation was the availability of English translations. Though it's beyond my ability to compile an exhaustive list of Chinese satirical writings (a WorldCat title search for 杂文 (*zawen*, barbed essay) alone yielded over 3,400 entries), in the appendix of the present book I add the sources I've saved over the years as well as most of those introduced in sixteen histories of and reference works in Chinese literature in English (including in translation).

Dr. Johnson says that in satire "wickedness or folly is censured." In *A Companion to Satire* Ruben Quintero adds that "without intentioned art there is no satire." Chinese critics who take a traditional approach see most literature as more or less political, and, as a result, tend to see a lot more satire (*fengci*) in classical sources than do critics who don't take that approach. Others disagree over the stylistic features of satire. In *A Brief History of Chinese Fiction* where Lu Xun first identified fiction of satire (*fengci xiaoshuo*) as a subgenre, he sees innuendo and subtlety as essential to satirical writing and says, "after *The Scholars* we can say there was no real satire." What later became known as the famous four late Qing satirical novels, *Guanchang xianxing ji* (Officialdom unmasked), *Ershi nian mudu zhi guai xianzhuang* (Bizarre happenings eyewitnessed over two decades), *Lao Can youji* (The travels of Lao Can) and *Nie hai hua* (A flower in a sea of sins), Lu Xun categories as *qianze xiaoshuo* (novels of condemnation). In this book I take an inclusive approach: not only are these four novels included (the last one in the appendix), works that are not primarily satirical but include obviously satirical passages or may be interpreted as satirical or as containing satirical elements are also included. (In fact, even Lu Xun did the last in his abovementioned work when he called Ren Jiji's *Renshi zhuan* (Ren the fox fairy) a satire.) Besides fiction, drama, poetry, sayings, essays and longer nonfiction are likewise included, leaving out cartoons (*manhua*), movies, crosstalk (*xiangsheng*) and skits (*xiaopin*).

The magnum opus of Sima Qian (Ssu-ma Ch'ien, Szuma Chien) has been partially translated into English at least six times since the 1960s, and I've selected quotes from three substantial translations. In *Vignettes from the Late Ch'ing: Bizarre Happenings Eyewitnessed over Two Decades*, where names are inconsistently rendered in Wade-Giles, suspected aberrations are marked "[*sic*]" on their first appearance only. Most footnotes and all the Chinese characters in the original are omitted. Publishers' names are abbreviated. Quote numbers instead of page numbers are used in the table of contents.

As always, my colleague Zack Hill helped me improve my writing. Thanks to Nik Money, the Western Program paid for the ISBN for the book. Don Moeller helped with pagination.

Bo Yang 柏楊

Sources and Quotations

***300 Song Lyrics*, trans. Xu Yuanchong, China Intercontinental Press/Zhonghua Book Co. (not the traditional anthology —Ed.), 2012**
1. While young, I knew no grief I could not bear;
I'd like to go upstair.
I'd like to go upstair
To write new verses with a false despair.

I know what grief is now that I am old;
I would not have it told.
I would not have it told,
But only say I'm glad that autumn's cold. (Xin Qiji, "Tune: Song of Ugly Slave," written on the wall on my way to Bushan, 177)

***ABC Dictionary of Chinese Proverbs*, John S. Rohsenow, U. of Hawai'i Press, 2002**
2. Drunkenness always has an awakening, [but] a money-grubber['s desire] knows no limits. (75)

3. Fame portends trouble for humans [just as] fattening does for pigs. (118)

4. People don't know the evil of their children, nor see the growing of the seedlings they plant. (ibid.)

***The Analects of Confucius*, Confucius, trans. Burton Watson, Columbia UP, 2007**
5. The Master said, Clever words and a pleasing countenance—little humaneness there! (1.3)

6. The Master said, I have never seen the person who loved virtue the way he loved physical beauty. (9.18)

7. The Master said, Women and petty persons are the hardest to look after. Treat them in a friendly manner, and they become impertinent; keep them at a distance, and they take offense. (17.25)

***The Annals of Lü Buwei: A Complete Translation and Study*, Lü Buwei, trans. John Knoblock and Jeffrey Riegel, Stanford UP, 2000**
8. A good coffin and vault will keep out insects and worms. But in the gross disorder of our vulgar age rulers have become ever more extravagant. Thus, in their burials their thoughts are directed, not at taking precautions on behalf of the dead, but at how the living can outdo each other. Extravagance is considered glorious, frugality demeaning. They are not motivated by what is of convenience to the dead, but are concerned with what the living might blame or praise. These are not the feelings of a loving parent or filial son. Although his father has died, a filial son's respect for him does not wane; although his son has died, a loving parent's love for him does not lessen.

When burying those one cherishes and respects, how can giving them what the living most desire bring them peaceful repose? (10/2.3, 228)

9. Today the world is in ever greater decline, and the Dao of the sage-kings has been cast aside and broken off. Rulers of the present are for the most part concerned with increasing their pleasures and joys, enlarging their bells and drums, and creating extravagant terraces, pavilions, gardens, and parks; this is why they expropriate the resources of others. They think nothing of working their people to death and so stir up their indignation. The aged and weak freeze or starve to death. The young and frail, even the robust and vigorous, are exhausted, which will lead to their death or enslavement. These rulers attack guiltless states in their pursuit of territory and execute innocent people in their search for profit. And although they desire that their ancestral temples be secure and their altars to the soil and grain not be endangered, are they not placed in even greater difficulty? (13/4.1, 289)

10. Now, however, when men occupy office, they become wild and disorderly; when they oversee goods, they covet them; when they are promoted into the ranks of the ruler's intimates, they become flatterers; and when they lead the multitudes they are cowardly. (13/6.1, 296)

11. When there is disorder, the stupid enjoy great favor. (14/7.1, 327)

12. King Xuan of Qi loved archery and enjoyed having others tell him how well he handled a taut bow. He usually used a bow that had a pull no more than three stones. He showed it to his attendants and let them test their strength by trying to pull it, but all of them stopped short of his mark, saying, "Not less than nine stones—who besides your majesty would be capable of using this bow?"

The truth of the matter was that the bow King Xuan used was no more than a three-stone bow, but to the end of his life he thought he could use a nine-stone one. How sad! Who but a candid scholar-knight is capable of not flattering a ruler? That the few candid scholar-knights of the world do not triumph over the many is the result of their numbers. Therefore, the trouble with the rulers of chaotic states is that they use three-stone bows but believe they are using nine-stone bows. (23/5.5, 601)

13. When the Fan family fled, one of the Hundred Clans found their bell, which he wanted to haul away, but it was too large to carry on his back. He struck the bell with a mallet to break it into pieces, but it resonated, *hwyang*! Fearful that others would hear the ring and try to take the bell from him, he quickly covered his ears. That he should dislike others' hearing the bell ring makes sense, but that he should dislike his hearing it himself is madness. Are not rulers who dislike hearing of their own errors like this? That they should hate others to hear of their errors also makes sense, but that they themselves should hate to hear of their own errors is madness. (24/3.4, 612–13)

14. The disciples and followers of Confucius and Mo Di fill the world, and they all provide it with instruction in the techniques of humaneness and morality. Nevertheless, these methods are not put into practice anywhere. If the teachers are unable to put their methods into practice, how can those they teach hope to do so? Why is this? Because the techniques of humaneness and morality are alien to human nature. Ordinary men who follow them are incapable of using what is alien to their

nature to overcome what inheres in it—how much less will this be true of rulers! Only with full comprehension of the true character of inborn nature and fate can the techniques of humaneness and morality be practiced by an individual. (25/3.4, 631)

***An Anthology of Chinese Literature: Beginnings to 1911*, ed. and trans. Stephen Owen, Norton, 1996**

15. Huge rat, huge rat,
eat my millet no more,
for three years I've fed you,
yet you pay me no heed. . . .

Huge rat, huge rat,
eat my wheat no more,
for three years I've fed you
and you show no gratitude. . . .

Huge rat, huge rat,
eat my sprouts no more
for three years I have fed you,
and you won't reward my toil. (*Classic of Poetry* CXIII "Huge Rat," 52–53)

16. Literary men have always insulted one another. Fu Yi [d. 90] and Ban Gu [32–92] were virtually brothers, but Ban Gu made fun of Fu Yi in a letter to his elder brother Ban Zhao, "Fu Yi got to be Imperial Librarian because he had a 'facility' in writing—that is, whenever he put his writing brush to paper, he couldn't stop himself."

Everyone is good at putting himself forward; but since literature is not restricted to one particular norm, few people can be good at everything. Therefore each person makes light of those things in which he is weakest by the criteria of his strengths. As the saying in the villages has it, "A worn-out broom is worth a thousand pieces of gold, so long as it belongs to me." This is a failure due to lack of self-awareness. (Cao Pi, "A Discourse on Literature (*Lun-wen*)," 360)

17. The salt merchant's wife
has silk and gold aplenty,
but she does not work at farming,
      nor does she spin the silk.
From north to south to east to west
      she never leaves her home,
wind and waters, her native land,
      her lodging is the boat.
Once she came from Yang-zhou,
      a humble family's child,
she married herself a merchant,
      a great one from Jiang-xi.
Her glinting hair-coils have grown rich,
      there golden pins abound,

her gleaming wrists have gotten plump,
        her silver bracelets tight.

On one side she shouts to her servants,
        on the other, yells at her maids,
and I ask you, how does it happen
        that you come to live like this?
Her husband has been a salt merchant
        for fifteen years now,
attached to no county or province,
        attached to the Emperor.
Every year when salt profits
        are to enter official hands,
the lesser part goes to officials,
        the greater part goes to himself.
Official profits are meager,
        private profits are rich,
the Secretary of Iron and Salt
        is far and does not know. (Bo Ju-yi, "Salt Merchant's Wife (in hatred of profiteers)," 501–02)

18. It is, indeed, a great amount of material. Yet catastrophe fell on Wang Ya and Yuan Zai alike: what did it matter that the one hoarded books and paintings while the other merely hoarded pepper? Chang-you and Yuan-kai both had a disease—it made no difference that the disease of one was a passion for money, and of the other, a passion for the transmission of knowledge and commentary. Although their reputations differed, they were the same in being deluded. (Li Qing-zhao, "Epilogue to *Records on Metal and Stone*," 591)

19. The Buddha was originally a tribesman from outlying regions. His language is incomprehensible to those who inhabit the heartland, and his clothes were of strange fashion. He did not speak the exemplary words of the early kings, and he did not wear the exemplary garb of the early kings. He did not understand the sense of right that exists between a ruler and his officers, nor the feelings between father and son. If he were still alive today and, on the orders of his own kingdom, were to come to an audience with Your Majesty in the capital, Your Majesty would tolerantly receive him, but with nothing more than a single meeting in Xuan-zheng Palace, the single feast to show politeness to a guest, and a single present of clothing. Then he would be escorted to the border under guard in order to keep him from leading the people astray.

    But now he has been dead for a very long time. Is it fitting that you order his dried and crumbling bone, this disgusting and baleful relic, to be brought into the imperial palace? Confucius said, "Respect gods and spirits, but keep far away from them." (Han Yu, "Memorial Discussing the Buddha's Bone," 600)

20. The fuban is a small insect that excels at carrying loads on its back. When it chances on something as it walks along, it immediately takes hold of it, and then, raising it up with its head, it loads the thing onto its back. The weight on its back gets increasingly heavy, but it will not stop what it does, even in dire straits. Its back is quite rough, so that the things it has accumulated do

not slip off. It eventually collapses and just lies there, unable to get up. Sometimes a person will feel pity for it and get rid of its load. But no sooner is it able to walk again than it takes hold of things just as it did before. It also likes to climb high places; and when it does so, it will continue to use every bit of its strength until it falls to the ground and dies. Those in our own times who lust to lay hold of things will never back away when they chance on possessions by which to enrich their household. They don't understand that it encumbers them; rather, they fear only that they won't accumulate enough. When they become weary and stumble, they are dismissed from office or sent into banishment. They even think that an ill has befallen them in this. If they can get up again, they will not forbear. Every day they think about how they can get a higher position and increase their income, and their greed for acquisition intensifies. As they draw near to falling from their perilous perch, they may consider those who have similarly perished before, yet they never take warning from the example. (Liu Zong-yuan, "The Story of the Fuban, or Pack Beetle," 617–18)

21. Glorious is our Mighty Yuan!—
all power is held by vile men.
The River Project and paper cash
        were root cause of our doom,
driving millions to insurrection.
Laws that govern slacken,
laws that punish, stern,
the common folk burn
        in rage:
men eat men,
cash buys cash,
things never before seen.
Thieves hold public office,
officials turn to thieves,
good men are confused with fools,
a sad state indeed. (Anon., "to 'Drunk in an Age of Peace'" (*Zui tai-ping*), 739)

22. Who has not wedded impetuously?
or leapt at the chance of married life?
and then who hasn't been carelessly dumped?
We are bubbles all, adrift on the waters,
        each one after another.
We make our own folks into enemies,
        so mad they won't see us again,
like sun and moon or opposing stars,
        each rising as the other sets,
when we get caught in men's snares.
They show every form of ardent passion,
thousands of kinds of love and care—
until, in the end,
        the slate is wiped bare. (Zhao Pan-er) (Guan Han-qing, *Rescuing One of the Girls* (*Jiu Feng-chen*), act 2, 755)

5

23. The brother-in-law of our ruler
        is ranked with the Three High Lords,
and I, of the Minister's household,
        hold an office of seventh degree. [*Greets* An]

24. Welcome, brother An! The Minister has accepted all your gifts and will have you meet with him in the Ministry office. (Zhang) (Hong Sheng, *The Palace of Lasting Life*, "Bribe (III)," 984–85)

25. Emperor: I had no idea that Yang Guo-zhong had started a feud or that An Lu-shan was
        plotting rebellion.
Guo (*sings*): Many a day had An Lu-shan
        hidden treason in his heart,
        and all in the whole world knew
                the shape of his treachery.
        Last year someone sent a letter to the throne giving Your Majesty evidence of An Lu-shan's
        treachery, but Your Majesty had the man put to death.
[*Sings*]
        Thereafter who would willingly face
                the headsman's ax
        to state the case to the throne? ("Gift of a Meal (XXVI)," 1050)

26. I am Lei Hai-qing, and I enjoyed the kindness of our Tian-bao Emperor, waiting at his service in the Pear Garden Academy. Then An Lu-shan unexpectedly rebelled, taking Chang-an; the Emperor went west to Sichuan. The civil and military officials who filled his court used to enjoy high positions and rich salaries, passing privilege on to their children and gaining fiefs for their wives; they enjoyed that splendor and became rich and noble—and each item of that came from the kindness of the court. But now every single one of them is hungry to stay alive and fears death. They turn their backs on what is right and forget what kindnesses they received, rushing in an unbroken stream to submit to their new ruler. They think only of their security and pleasures in the present moment and pay no heed to the disgrace of their names for all time. It makes one feel ashamed and angry! Even though I am only a musician, I could never do anything so shamefully self-serving. ("Denouncing the Rebel (XXVIII)," 1054–55)

"Big Ruan and Little Ruan," Shen Congwen, trans. William MacDonald, in *Imperfect Paradise: Stories by Shen Congwen*, ed. Jeffrey Kinkley, trans. Jeffrey Kinkley, et al., U. of Hawai'i Press, 1995

27. Little Ruan looked at the immaculately dressed Big Ruan and just smiled. Time had separated the two men. He didn't know why, but in his heart he had always had a little contempt for his young uncle. The ancestors had given Big Ruan an estate, he thought, but they hadn't given him a very good brain. All that cleverness was only good for wasting the small legacy the ancestors had left him. He was constantly primping and preening, just like a woman, and he always wore scent. All this effort just to please a vain and licentious girl who considered herself attractive to the opposite sex. To please a girl! His only other life's aim was to eat and drink. And so he lived in drunkenness and befuddlement. He wasn't of much consequence to the rest of the world.

The Book of Lieh-tzu: A Classic of the Tao, Lieh-tzu, trans. A. C. Graham, Columbia UP, 1990

28. There was a man who lost his axe, and suspected the boy next door. He watched the boy walking: he had stolen the axe! His expression, his talk, his behaviour, his manner, everything about him betrayed that he had stolen the axe.

Soon afterwards the man was digging in his garden and found the axe. On another day he saw the boy next door again; nothing in his behaviour and manner suggested that he would steal an axe. (180)

29. Once there was a man of Ch'i who wanted gold. At dawn he put on his coat and cap and set out for market. He went to the stall of a dealer in gold, snatched his gold and made off. The police caught him and questioned him.

'Why did you snatch somebody else's gold in front of so many people?'
'At the time when I took it, I did not see the people, I only saw the gold.' (180–81)

The Book of Songs, trans. Arthur Waley, ed. with additional translations by Joseph R. Allen, Grove, 1996

30. We were led by Sun Zi-zhong
To subdue Chen and Song.
He does not bring us home;
My heart is sad within.

Here we stop, here we stay,
Here we lose horses
And here find them again
Down among the woods.

"For good or ill, in death as in life;
This is the oath I swear with you.
I take your hand
As token that I will grow old along with you."

Alas for our bond!
It has not lasted even for our lifetime.
Alas for our troth!
You did not trust me. (no. 31, "They Beat Their Drums," stanzas 2–5)

31. Look at the rat; he has a skin.
A man without dignity,
A man without dignity,
What is he doing, that he does not die?

Look at the rat; he has teeth.
A man without poise,
A man without poise,
What is he waiting for, that he does not die?

Look at the rat; he has limbs.
A man without manners,
A man without manners*
Had best quickly die. (*43fn1: But *li* includes a great deal that we should call religion; for example, sacrificing at the right time.) (no. 52, "Look at the Rat.")

32. *Suk, suk* goes that row of bustards;
They have settled on the mulberry clump.
But the king's business never ends;
I cannot plant my rice and spiked millet.
Then how shall my father and mother be fed?
O blue Heaven so far off,
When will things go back to their wonted ways? (no. 121, "The Bustard's Plumes," stanza 3)

33. "Kio" sings the oriole
As it lights on the thorn bush.
Who went with Duke Mu to the grave?
Yan-xi of the clan Zi-ju.
Now this Yan-xi
Was the pick of all our men;
But as he drew near the tomb-hole
His limbs shook with dread.
That blue one, Heaven,
Takes all our good men.
Could we but ransom him
There are a hundred would give their lives. (no. 131, "The Oriole," stanza 1)

34. By the Tomb Gate are thorn-trees;
With an axe they are felled.
Man, you are not good,
And the people of this country know it,
Know it, but do nothing to check you;
For very long it has been so. (no. 141, "Tomb Gate," stanza 1)

35. We plucked the bracken, plucked the bracken
While the young shoots were springing up.
Oh, to go back, go back!
The year is ending.
We have no house, no home
Because of the Xian-yun.
We cannot rest or bide
Because of the Xian-yun. (no. 167, "Plucking Bracken," stanza 1)

36. Minister of War,
Truly you are not wise.

Why should you roll us from misery to misery?
We have mothers who lack food. (no. 185, "Ministers of War," stanza 3)

37. I went into the country;
I plucked the pokeweed.
You thought nothing of the old marriage—
Found for yourself a new mate.
Not for her wealth, oh no!
But merely for a change. (no. 188, "I Went into the Country," stanza 3)

38. Mighty Heaven is now unfair,
Our king is not at peace,
He does not take heed his own heart,
And turns on those who complain. (no. 191, "High-Crested Southern Hills," stanza 9)

39. When my parents gave birth to me,
What brought on this affliction?
Why not before my coming?
Why not after?
First they shower me with sweet words,
Then their words are vile.
More and more I have a grieved heart,
And for this I am abused.

My grieved heart is helpless,
To think of me without sustenance.
And people quite innocent
Are sentenced to be slaves and servants.
Oh, take pity on us people,
Where will sustenance be secured?
Look, the ominous raven swoops,
On whose house will he alight? (no. 192, "The First Month," stanzas 2–3)

40. Broad and vast is mighty Heaven,
Yet it keeps its grace from us,
But rather brings death and famine,
War and destruction to all the states.
Foreboding Heaven is a cruel affliction,
It does not ponder, does not plan.
It pays no attention to the guilty,
Who have admitted their crimes.
But the ones who are innocent,
These, without exception, suffer. (no. 194, "Rain Without Limit," stanza 1)

41. Level and easy was the way of Zhou,
But now it is over-grown with weeds.

My heart is filled with grief and pain,
My ponderings make me sick of heart.
With deep sighs, I need to sleep;
It's not just grief, but also age.
Indeed my heart is grieved;
My head pounds, fevers rage. (no. 197, "Wings Flapping," stanza 2)

42. My lord had many covenants made,
And for that the disorder deepened.
My lord has followed slanderous thieves,
And with that the disorder turned mean.
The words of those thieves are sweet,
And with them the disorder is fed,
They are not doing their duty,
But instead are the king's affliction. (no. 198, "Clever Words," stanza 3)

43. Jibber-jabber, blither-blather!
Their idea of "counsel" is to slander men.
And if you speak with any caution
They say that you are not loyal. (no. 200, "The Chief of Attendants," stanza 3)

44. Buzz, buzz the bluebottles
That have settled on the hedge,
Oh, my blessed lord,
Do not believe the slanders that are said. (no. 219, "The Bluebottles," stanza 1)

45. Grave and dignified manners
Are the helpmates of power.
Men indeed have a saying,
"There is none so wise but has his follies."
But ordinary people's follies
Are but sicknesses of their own.
It is the wise man's follies
That are a rampant pest. (no. 256, "Grave," stanza 1)

A Book to Burn and a Book to Keep (Hidden): Selected Writings of Li Zhi, Li Zhi, ed. and trans. Rivi Handler-Spitz, Pauline C. Lee, and Haun Saussy, Columbia UP, 2016
46. Alas! In the whole world, among all sentient beings, there are only shortsighted people with pressing desires; their appetites go no further than that. Are there any who have attained enlightenment? How difficult it is to make people long for what Confucius and Yan Hui ate and drank! I say that even if Confucius were to reappear on earth a thousand years from now and use his skill at seduction on such people, he would find it impossible to alter their appetites to make them correspond to what I eat and drink. (Selections from A Book to Burn, "A Letter in Reply to Provincial Officer Liu," trans. Rivi Handler-Spitz, 17)

47. But people today who take themselves for Confucius and want to seduce others and make followers of them are just absurd. Why? Because even Confucius had no success beyond Yan Hui. . . . Having been born after the days of Confucius, I find scholarly discussions of no benefit whatever. Even if I had not aspired to shave off my hair and leave my family to become a monk, or to seek hermits and transcendents as my companions, I would have been compelled to do so. So is there anyone at all with whom I, born in this era, may eat and drink? No, there is truly no one at all fit to eat and drink with me. (18)

48. Though the space within the four seas is great, finding a friend is difficult: great men are not numerous. Those who love learning are even more rare. ("Reply to Censor Geng [Letter 8]," trans. Timothy Brook, 35)

49. At this time, a powerful but corrupt official was in office. When money wasn't coming into his hands, he would shake down the wealthy families. Subordinating everything else to canal-digging projects, he used up all the water from the springs to feed the canals and did not permit even half a drop to be diverted. The Recluse went to meet with this individual. Although the Recluse ardently pleaded on behalf of the local inhabitants, his requests were not granted. But because the Recluse himself had only a few acres, the official said he could have water diverted just to his fields.

The Recluse replied, "Alas! Heavens! How could I bear to sit and see the entire city and ten thousand acres of land dry up, and only my few fields irrigated and flourishing! I cannot accept this at all. I beg you to heed my request!"

He then returned to his natal home.

That year's harvest was extremely meager. The plot of land acquired by the Recluse barely yielded a few bushels of weeds. His eldest daughter had long endured difficult times. She ate the weeds as if she were eating grain. His second and third daughters were unable to gulp down the weeds and soon both, so young, had fallen ill and died. ("A Sketch of Zhuowu: Written in Yunnan," trans. Pauline C. Lee, 80–81)

50. When humans first came into existence, there were simply two forces—Yin and Yang—and two destinies, male and female; in the beginning there was no so-called One or Principle; certainly there did not exist a Supreme Ultimate! Looking at the matter today, as for this so-called One, indeed, what is this thing? And what is referred to as Principle: where does it reside? And what we call Supreme Ultimate: what does it refer to? If Two come from One, then where does One come from? A one and another one make two. Principle and qi are two; Yin-Yang and the Supreme Ultimate are two; the Supreme Ultimate and the Ultimateless [$wuji$] are two. No matter how many times you look at the matter, there is nothing that arises without its paired term. Yet some who have never seen this so-called One nonetheless hastily and rashly speak of it! ("Discussion on Husband and Wife: Reflections after Long Contemplation," trans. Pauline C. Lee, 100)

51. If a work possesses a tight structure, if the couplets are perfectly aligned, if the writing is grounded in solid logic and is in harmony with established models, if the beginning and end echo each other, and the abstract and concrete elements are in balance—all these various illusory criteria are used to discuss literature. But such criteria cannot be used to discuss the most exquisite literature under heaven. ("On Miscellaneous Matters," trans. Pauline C. Lee, 103)

52. Since the heart-mind is made up of what one sees and hears and Principles of the Way, what is spoken then are words that derive entirely from what one has seen and heard and from the Principles of the Way; one's words do not flow directly from the childlike heart-mind. Though these words may be artful, what do they have to do with oneself? How could such a situation lead to anything other than phony people speaking phony words, performing phony actions, and producing phony writings? Once a person is a phony, everything he does is phony. As a consequence, if one speaks phony words to a phony person, the phony person is pleased; if one talks about phony matters with a phony person, the phony person is pleased; if one discusses phony literature with a phony person, the phony person is pleased. When everything is phony, everyone is pleased. And when the entire theater is filled with phonies, how can a short person in the audience discriminate between real and fake?

So even the most exquisite writing in the world can be buried by phony people and never even seen by later generations. Is this all that rare? Why does this happen? All the most exquisite literature in the world flows directly from the childlike heart-mind. ("Explanation of the Childlike Heart-Mind," trans. Pauline C. Lee and Rivi Handler-Spitz, 108)

53. As for the Six Classics, the *Analects*, and the *Mencius*, if they are not words of overdone reverence from official historians, they are phrases of bloated praise from loyal subjects. If not one or the other, then they are what misguided followers and dim-witted disciples wrote down of what they *recalled* their teacher had said. What they wrote had a beginning but was missing an ending; or the followers remembered the conclusion but forgot the introduction. These disciples put down in writing whatever they happened to see. Later scholars did not scrutinize these writings. They simply declared that these words came directly from the mouths of sages and decided to establish them as great classics. Who knows whether more than half these writings are *not* words from the mouths of sages?

Even *if* these words are those of the sages, still, they were uttered in response to a specific situation. This is much like the case of prescribing a medication for a particular illness, applying a specific remedy depending on the circumstances in order to cure this dim-witted disciple or that misguided follower. The medicine prescribed depends on the illness; surely there is no fixed and unchanging prescription. Given this, how could we hastily accept these writings as the perfected doctrine for endless generations? And so, the Six Classics, the *Analects*, and the *Mencius* have become nothing more than a crib sheet for those belonging to the School of Principle, a fountainhead for phonies. It would be utterly impossible to describe such writings with the label of "childlike heart-mind." (109–10)

54. But in this world, very few people possess genuine talent and intelligence. ("On Loftiness and Cleanliness," trans. Rivi Handler-Spitz, 123)

55. Writing when you aren't indignant is like shivering when you're not cold, groaning and moaning when you aren't sick. Although you could write *something*, would it really be worth reading? ("Preface to *The Loyal and Righteous Outlaws of the Marsh*," trans. Huiying Chen and Drew Dixon, 125)

56. And yet I regret that people who study the Dao suffer from the malady of loving themselves more than they love the Dao. Because of this, they do not comprehend the value of the wisdom entrusted to them by the ancients. Instead, they scheme only for their own profit and interest. Their

sickness is that they respect reputation but do not respect themselves, and so they disregard the painful fact that their sons and grandsons are sinking into moral decline. Instead, they consider it their chief responsibility to steer clear of suspicion and slander. Alas! Establishing their hearts and minds in such a manner diminishes the Dao, it does not transmit it. Through such actions they forfeit their true selves; they do not actualize themselves. ("In Memoriam, Master Wang Longxi," trans. Rivi Handler-Spitz, 148)

57. In this world true friendship has been lost for a long time. Why should this be so? The whole world is fond of profit; no one is fond of righteousness. People who love righteousness view death as no different from life. To this sort of person one could entrust a child or an orphan; one could even entrust one's family or one's own life—how could a righteous friend decline? But those who are fond of profit lead lives no different from death; they reach out their arms to snatch food away from others, and if they see a person in difficulty, they rain stones upon him to stop up his mouth—these are the kinds of acts of which they're capable.

All the people who pass for friends today lead lives no different from death. The only reason for this is that they are fond of profit, not friendship. In this day and age, is there anyone fond of the righteousness between friends? Since there have never been any friends fond of righteousness, it is fair to say that friendship has never existed. If we were to serve our ruler in the same [false] manner [in which we treat our friends], on whom could the ruler rely? ("On Friendship," Rivi Handler-Spitz, 207–08)

58. The only people who have been able to move beyond the sphere of reputation and profit and to conceive of themselves in terms other than reputation and profit are the three great sages Confucius, Old Master Li, and the Śākyamuni Buddha. Apart from them, everyone else is after either profit or reputation. . . . A man who at seventy-three instructs others not to pursue profit is just as foolish as a man who at seventy-six pursues both profit and reputation. (Selections from *Another Book to Burn*, "A Reply to Li Shilong," trans. Rivi Handler-Spitz, 248)

59. Most people are either extremely arrogant or utterly obsequious; if they're not flaunting their intelligence, they're bumbling fools. ("Letter to a Friend," trans. Rivi Handler-Spitz, 257)

60. I am old and will die soon, yet time and time again I have suffered from these symptoms of illness [i.e., the moral shortcomings of arrogance, ambition, and thoughtlessness]. No wonder that so often I have been the victim of others' bullying and oppression. How could people like Yang Dingjian—whose resolve surpasses mine yet whose knowledge and insight lag behind mine—not diligently carry with them [Laozi's words] throughout their lives! ("A Brief Introduction to a Selection of Daoist Teachings," trans. Jennifer Eichman, 266)

The Chronicle of the Three Kingdoms (220–265) (Chapters 69–78 from the* Tzŭ chih t'ung chien*), Sima Guang, trans. Achilles Fang, online version transcribed by Jordan, the-scholars.com, 2004
61. During the Zhengshi period (240–249 A.D.), Xiahou Xuan, He Yan and Deng Yang all enjoyed brilliant reputations. They wanted to make friends with the shangshu lang Fu Jia, but Fu Jia would not accept their friendship. Fu Jia's friend Xun Can wondered at this and asked him about it. Fu Jia said, "As for Taichu (Xiaohou Xuan), his aims are bigger than his capacities; he is able to

gather empty fame around himself, but he lacks real talent. As for He Pingshu (He Yan), his talk is far-ranging, but his feelings are close-in. He is good at argument, but lacks sincerity. He is one who, as the saying has it, with his sharp mouth overthrows kingdoms. As for Deng Xuanmao (Deng Yang), he is always doing but never accomplishing. From the outside he covets name and gain; he lacks the qualifications. He prizes those who agree with him and hates those who differ. He is free with his words and jealous of others getting ahead of him. Being free with his words, he will have many enemies; jealous of others getting ahead of him, he will have no intimates. As far as I can observe of these three men, they will all ruin their families. Even keeping my distance from them, I fear calamity may reach me. Should I then cultivate their intimacy?" (First Year of Zhengyuan (254 A.D.) (Shu: Seventeenth Year of Yanxi) (Wu: First year of Wufeng), sec. 13)

62. Fu Jia was not on good terms with Li Feng either. He said to his intimate friends, "Li Feng is an elegant fake, full of doubts; he prides himself on his petty cleverness, but is blind to what is really needed in exigencies. If he is charged with important duties, his death is inevitable."
(sec. 14)

Chuang-tzǔ: The Inner Chapters, Chuang-tzǔ, trans. A. C. Graham, Hackett, 2001
63. When Chuang Chou was roaming inside the fenced preserve at Tiao-ling, he noticed a strange magpie coming from the south, with wings seven feet wide and eyes a full inch across. It brushed against his forehead and perched in a chestnut grove.

'What bird is this?' said Chuang Chou. 'With wings so huge it doesn't fly away, with eyes so big it didn't notice.'

He hitched up his robe and quickened his step, and with crossbow at the ready waited to take aim.

He noticed a cicada which had just found a beautiful patch of shade and had forgotten what could happen to it. A mantis hiding behind the leaves grabbed at it, forgetting at the sight of gain that it had a body of its own. The strange magpie in his turn was taking advantage of that, at the sight of profit forgetful of its truest prompting.

'Hmm!' said Chuang Chou uneasily. 'It is inherent in things that they are ties [*sic*] to each other, that one kind calls up another.' . . .

'In caring for the body I have been forgetting what can happen to me. I have been looking at reflections in muddy water, have gone astray from the clear pool. Besides, I have heard the Master say "If it's the custom there, do as you're told." Now when I wandered in Tiao-ling I forgot what could happen to me; when the strange magpie brushed against my forehead I strayed into the chestnut grove and forgot my truest prompting, and the gamekeeper in the chestnut grove took me for a criminal. That is why I am gloomy.' (*Chuang-tzǔ,* chapter 20) (pt. 3, ch. 1, 118)

64. It is when it is to be found in a book that the world values the Way. A book is no more than sayings, but there is value in sayings; what is valuable in them is the thought. A thought is about something; what the thought is about is untransmittable in words, yet for the sake of it the world values the words and transmits the book. Even though the world values them, to me they seem valueless, because what is valued in them is not what is valuable.

The visible to sight is shape and colour, the audible to hearing is name and sound; how sad it is then that worldly people think shape and colour, name and sound, sufficient means to grasp the identity of that! If shape, colour, name, sound, are really inadequate means to grasp its identity, then, since knowers do not say and sayers do not know, how would the world recognise it? (*Chuang-tzŭ,* chapter 13) (ch. 3, 139)

65. An even measure is a blessing, excess is an injury; that is so of all things, but most of all of possessions. Now in the case of the rich man, his ears dote on the sounds of bells and drums, flutes and pipes, his mouth drools over the tastes of fine meats and wines, stirring his fancy until he overlooks and neglects his serious business. You can call that "lassitude". He is choked and flooded by the swelling of his energies, it is like climbing a slope with a heavy load on his back. You can count that as "strain". Out of greed for riches he chooses to risk his health, out of greed for mastery he chooses to wear himself out; when he rests at home he spoils himself, and as his body gets fatter his temper gets worse. That comes under "ill health". His end in life is desire for wealth, the urge for profit, so when his coffers are as tight as the stones in a wall he doesn't know how to do anything else, however full they are he won't leave off. That amounts to "ignominy". With more wealth in store than he can use, he clings to it and won't part with a penny, his heart is full of stresses and cares, he cannot stop seeking more and more. Put that down as "anxiety". At home he is suspicious of being plundered by cadgers and pilferers, abroad is in dread of being murdered by bandits; at home he is surrounded by towers and moats, abroad does not dare to walk alone. That comes under the heading of "fear". (Temperate) (*Chuang-tzŭ,* chapter 29) (pt. 5, ch. 2, 243)

A Collection of Chinese Proverbs, trans. and arr. William Scarborough, American Presbyterian Mission Press, 1875
66. If you would not be cheated ask the price at three shops. (29)

67. The melon seller declares his melons sweet. (ibid.)

68. To pretend that the house leaks in order to defraud the landlord of his rent. (46)

69. To guess a superior man's mind by a mean man's heart. (105)

70. To seek the ass you're riding on. (106)

71. To ask a blind man the way. (107)

72. To look for bones in an egg. (108)

73. His heart is loftier than his destiny. (113)

74. Man resembles the stump of a tree;—
Completely dependent on clothing is he. (206)

75. A shameless man is ready for anything. (213)

76. The skin of his face is as thick as a city wall. (ibid.)

77. Clever men are sometimes the dupes of their own cleverness. (216)

78. A good drum does not require hard striking. (217)

79. The self-conceited come to grief; the boastful are but fools. (219)

80. His mouth is sweet as honey; his heart as venomous as a snake. (229)

81. The friendship of superior men is like water thin and pure;
Without constant interchange of feasts mean men's friendship can't endure. (235)

82. There are plenty of men, but few superior men. (ibid.)

83. The superior man eats for the taste; the mean man gorges himself to death and is not satisfied. (238)

84. Propriety rules the superior man; law rules the mean man. (ibid.)

85. He whose virtues exceed his talents is the superior man; he whose talents exceed his virtues is the mean man. (ibid.)

86. Nine women in ten are jealous. (241)

87. I guess that a good-looking woman needs no rouge to make her pretty. (242)

88. There is no such poison in the green snake's mouth or the hornet's sting, as in a woman's heart. (243)

89. With one smile she overthrows a city; with another, a kingdom. (244)

90. When you see into man's disposition, you perceive that all is false. (254)

91. To deceive the good and fear the bad. (291)

92. It is not beauty that beguiles men; men beguile themselves. (ibid.)

93. There is no one to sweep a common hall. (302)

***The Complete Works of Han Fei Tzŭ: A Classic of Chinese Political Science*, Han Fei Tzŭ, trans. W. K. Liao, A. Probsthian, 1959**
94. Thy servant, Fei, is by no means diffident of speaking. As to why he has to hesitate in speaking: if his speeches are compliant and harmonious, magnificent and orderly, he is then regarded as ostentatious and insincere; if his speeches are sincere and courteous, straightforward and careful, he is then regarded as awkward and unsystematic; if his speeches are widely cited and subtly composed, frequently illustrated and continuously analogized, he is then regarded as empty and unpractical; if his speeches summarize minute points and present general ideas, being thus plain and concise, he is then regarded as simple and not discerning; if his speeches are very personally observing and well-versed in the inner nature of mankind, he is then regarded as self-assuming

and self-conceited; if his speeches are erudite and profound, he is then regarded as boastful but useless; if his speeches touch the details of house-keeping and estimate each item in terms of numerals, he is then regarded as vulgar; if his speeches are too much concerned with worldly affairs and not offensive in wording, he is then regarded as a coward and a flatterer; if his speeches are far from commonplace and contrary to human experience, he is then regarded as fantastic; if his speeches are witty and eloquent and full of rhetorical excellences, he is then regarded as flippant; if he discards all literary forms of expression and speaks solely of the naked facts, he is then regarded as rustic; and should he quote the *Books of Poetry and History* from time to time and act on the teachings of the former sages, he is then regarded as a book chantor. These things explain the reason why thy servant, Fei, is diffident in speaking and worried about speaking. (v. 1, bk. 1, ch. 3, "On the Difficulty in Speaking: A Memorial," 23–24)

95. [A]ll stupid scholars in the world do not know the actual conditions of order and chaos but chatter nonsense and chant too many hackneyed old books to disturb the government of the present age. Though their wisdom and thought are not sufficient to avoid pitfalls, they dare to absurdly reproach the upholders of tact. Whoever listens to their words, will incur danger. Whoever employs their schemes, will invite confusion. Such is the greatest height of stupidity as well as the greatest extreme of calamity. Though they gain fame for discussion and persuasion just as the upholders of tact do, yet in reality the former are as far apart from the latter as a distance of thousands of li. That is to say, the similarity is nominal but the difference is actual. (bk. 4, ch. 14, "Ministers Apt to Betray, Molest, or Murder the Ruler," 123–24)

96. Who does private favours to old acquaintances, is called a kind-hearted *alter ego*. Who distributes alms with public money, is called a benevolent man. Who makes light of bounties but thinks much of himself, is called a superior man. Who strains the law to shield his relatives, is called a virtuous man. Who deserts official posts for cultivating personal friendships, is called a chivalrous man. Who keeps aloof from the world and avoids all superiors, is called lofty. Who quarrels with people and disobeys orders, is called an unyielding hero. Who bestows favours and attracts the masses of people, is called a popular idol.

However, the presence of kind-hearted men implies the existence of culprits among the magistrates; the presence of benevolent men, the losses of public funds; the presence of superior men, the difficulty in employing the people; the presence of virtuous men, the violation of laws and statutes; the appearance of chivalrous men, vacancies of official posts; the appearance of lofty men, the people's neglect of their proper duties; the emergence of unyielding heroes, the inefficacy of orders; and the appearance of popular idols, the isolation of the sovereign from the subjects. (v. 2, ch. 47, "Eight Fallacies," 248)

***Courtier and Commoner in Ancient China: Selections from the* History of the Former Han, Pan Ku, trans. Burton Watson, Columbia UP, 1974**

97. At this time Tung-fang Shuo was in attendance, and he stepped forward with the following remonstrance: "I have heard that Heaven responds to humility and quietude—responds by sending down good fortune. It likewise responds to pride and extravagance—by sending down prodigies! Now Your Majesty has built story on story of verandahs and terraces, fearful only that they would not be high enough; has marked off lands for shooting and hunting, fearful only that they would not be vast enough. If Heaven manifests no unusual change in the face of this, then why not take over the entire capital area and make it into a park? Why confine yourself to the region of Hu-tu?

But if such luxury and extravagance, such overstepping of bounds, should draw a response from Heaven, then, small though the Shang-lin area may be, I fear it will still be too big!" ("Han shu 65: The Biography of Tung-fang Shuo," 85)

98. At this time there were many talented and worthy men at court. The emperor continued to question Shuo, saying, "Nowadays we have men like Prime Minister Kung-sun, Lord Ni, Tung Chung shu, Hsia-hou Shih-ch'ang, Ssu-ma Hsiang-ju, Wu-ch'iu Shou-wang, Chu-fu Yen, Chu Mai-ch'en, Chuang Chu, Chi An, Chiao Ts'ang, Chung Chün, Yen An, Hsü Yüeh, and Ssu-ma Ch'ien, all of great wisdom and understanding, with superlative talent in letters and learning. Looking at yourself, how do you think you compare?"

Shuo replied, "When I see them clacking teeth and fangs, puffing out jowls, spluttering from the mouth, craning necks and chins, lining up flank by thigh, pairing off buttock bones, snaking their way along, mincing side by side in crook-backed ranks, then I say to myself, Shuo, you may not be much, but you're still equal to all these gentlemen put together!" (95–96)

***Dictionary of Classic Chinese Quotations with English Translation*, editor in chief, Qian Housheng, Nanjing UP, 2010**
99. Tyranny is fiercer than a tiger. (Confucius, 195)

100. Things that are too high fall down easily; things that are too white stain easily. (Fan Ye, 409)

101. He who knows the past but not the present is called a pedant. . . . He who knows the present but not the past is blind. (Wang Chong, 454)

***A Dream of Red Mansions*, Tsao Hsueh-chin and Kao Ngo, trans. Yang Hsien-yi and Gladys Yang, Foreign Languages Press, 1978–80**
102. All men long to be immortals,
Yet to riches and rank each aspires;
The great ones of old, where are they now?
Their graves are a mass of briars.

All men long to be immortals,
Yet silver and gold they prize
And grub for money all their lives
Till death seals up their eyes.

All men long to be immortals
Yet dote on the wives they've wed,
Who swear to love their husband evermore
But remarry as soon as he's dead.

All men long to be immortals
Yet with getting sons won't have done.
Although fond parents are legion,
Who ever saw a really filial son? (v. 1, ch. 1)

103. A centipede dies but never falls down, as the old saying goes. Although they're not as prosperous as before, they're still a cut above ordinary official families. Their households are increasing and their commitments are growing all the time, while masters and servants alike are so used to lording it in luxury that not one of them thinks ahead. They squander money every day and are quite incapable of economizing. Outwardly they may look as grand as ever, but their purses are nearly empty. That's not their worst trouble, though. Who would've thought that each new generation of this noble and scholarly clan is inferior to the last. (Tzu-hsing) (ch. 2)

104. Then, deferentially, the attendant perched sideways on the edge of a chair. And Yu-tsun asked why he had stopped him from issuing the warrants.

"Now that Your Honour's come to this post," said the attendant, "surely you've copied out the Officials' Protective Charm for this province?"

"Officials' Protective Charm? What do you mean?"

"Don't tell me you've never heard of it? In that case you won't keep your job long. All local officials nowadays keep a secret list of the most powerful, wealthy and high-ranking families in their province. Each province has such a list. Because if unknowingly you offend one of these families, you may lose not only your post but your life as well. That's why it's called a Protective Charm. This Hsueh family mentioned just now is one Your Honour can't afford to offend. There's nothing difficult about this case, but out of deference to them it was never settled by your predecessor." (ch. 4)

105. "There's much in what you say. But a man's life is involved. Moreover, I've been re-instated by the Emperor's favour and am in fact beginning a new life. I should be doing my utmost to show my gratitude. How can I flout the law for private considerations? I really can't bring myself to do such a thing." (Yu-tsun)

The attendant sneered: "Your Honour is right, of course. But that won't get you anywhere in the world today. Remember the old sayings; 'A gentleman adapts himself to circumstances' and 'The superior man is one who pursues good fortune and avoids disaster.' If you do as you just said, not only will you be unable to repay the Emperor's trust, you may endanger your own life into the bargain." (ibid.)

106. Too much cunning in plotting and scheming
Is the cause of her own undoing;
While yet living her heart is broken
And after death all her subtlety comes to nothing.
A rich house, all its members at peace,
Is ruined at last and scattered;
In vain her anxious thought for half a lifetime,
For like a disturbing dream at dead of night,
Like the thunderous collapse of a great mansion,
Or the flickering of a lamp that gutters out,
Mirth is suddenly changed to sorrow.
Ah, nothing is certain in the world of men. ("Ruined by Cunning," ch. 5)

107. You're such an exceptional woman, aunt, that even men in official belts and caps are no match for you. Is it possible you don't know the sayings that "the moon waxes only to wane, water brims

only to overflow," and "the higher the climb the harder the fall"? Our house has prospered for nearly a hundred years. If one day it happens that at the height of good fortune the "tree falls and the monkeys scatter" as the old saying has it, then what will become of our cultured old family? (Ko-ching to Hsi-feng) (ch. 13)

108. "Well, I understand that General Yun the Military Governor of Changan is on friendly terms with your family. If Lady Wang would get His Lordship to write to General Yun, asking him to have a word with the inspector, I'm sure he'd drop the suit. And the Changs would gladly give anything—even their whole fortune—in return for this favour." (the Abbess)

"There shouldn't be any great difficulty about this," rejoined Hsi-feng. "But Her Ladyship doesn't trouble herself with such matters."

"In that case, madam, could you attend to it?"

"I'm neither short of money nor do I meddle with affairs of this sort."

The abbess' face fell. After a short pause she observed with a sigh, "Well, the Changs know that I'm appealing to your family. If you do nothing, they won't realize that you can't be troubled and don't want the money—it would look as if you can't even handle such a trifling business."

This put Hsi-feng on her mettle. "You know me," she replied. "I've never believed all that talk about Hell and retribution. I do what I please and am always as good as my word. Let them bring me three thousand taels and I'll see to this for them."

"Very good!" cried the abbess, overjoyed. "That's easy."

I'm not one of your go-betweens just out for money," said Hsi-feng. "These three thousand taels will just cover the expenses of the servants I send out and reward them for their trouble. I myself don't want a cent. I could lay my hands on *thirty* thousand."

"Of course, madam. Will you do us this favour, then, tomorrow?"

"Can't you see how busy I am, needed right and left? But since I've told you I'll do it, of course I'll settle it for you speedily."

"A little thing like this might throw other people into a fearful flurry, but I know you'd have no trouble handling bigger things than this, madam. As the proverb says, 'The abler a man, the busier he gets.' It's because you're so capable that Her Ladyship leaves everything to you. But you mustn't wear yourself out."

This flattery made Hsi-feng forget her exhaustion and start chatting more cheerfully. (ch. 15)

109. Virtuous maids have always harboured grief,
And charming wives since of old have known jealousy. (ch. 21)

110. "There's a sameness about all these tales," complained the old lady. "And they're so stereotyped—all about talented scholars and lovely ladies. Fancy describing girls who behave so badly as fine young ladies! Why, they're nothing of the sort. They're always introduced as girls from cultured families whose fathers are invariably high officials or prime ministers. In that case, an only daughter would be treasured and brought up as a real fine young lady, well-versed in literature and a model of propriety; yet her first glimpse of a handsome man, whether a relative or family friend, sets her thoughts running on marriage. She forgets her parents then and gets up to all sorts of devilry, behaving quite unlike a fine lady. If she carries on like that she's surely no lady, no matter how her head is crammed with learning. If a man whose head is crammed with learning becomes a thief, does the court spare him on account of his talent? So these story-tellers contradict

themselves.

"Besides, not only would the daughter of a good scholar-official family be well-educated and a model of propriety—so would her mother. And even if her father had retired, a big family like that would have plenty of nurses and maids to look after the girl. How is it that in all these stories, when such things happen, no one has any inkling of it except the girl herself and one trusted maid? What are all the others doing, I'd like to know? Isn't that contradictory?" (v. 2, ch. 54)

111. There's no lack of young lordlings, but they all want three wives and five concubines and their affections change from one day to the next. They may bring home a wife as lovely as a fairy, yet after four or five nights they cast her off, treating her like an enemy for the sake of a concubine or a slave girl. If her family's large and powerful, that's not so bad; and for someone like you [Tai-yu], miss, so long as the old lady lives you'll be all right. Once she's gone, you'll have to put up with ill treatment. So it's important to make up your mind. You've sense enough to understand the saying, "Ten thousand taels of gold are easier come by than an understanding heart." (Tzu-chuan) (ch. 57)

112. Chia Chen and Chia Jung, by duty bound to keep vigil by the coffin and mourn, nevertheless seized the chance once the guests had gone to fool around with old Mrs. Yu's two daughters. Pao-yu, wearing mourning, also went every day to the Ning Mansion, not returning to the Garden till the evening after the guests had left. (ch. 64)

113. Of course Lord Chen's to blame too. Still, it's because our master is so debauched that it's easy for people to tempt him. As the proverb says, "If an ox doesn't want to drink, you can't force it to." (Hsi-feng) (ch. 67)

114. Now this Miss Hsia, who had just turned seventeen, was quite good-looking and had some education. As regards ability and craftiness, she took after Hsi-feng. In one respect only had she been unlucky. Because her father had died when she was a child, and she had no brothers either, her widowed mother had spoilt this only daughter, doting on her and falling in with all her whims. Inevitably, this over-indulgence had made her like the brigand Tao Chih of old: she had as high an opinion of herself as if she were a goddess, and treated others like dirt. In appearance pretty as a flower, at heart she was a termagant. At home she had vented her temper on her maids, for ever cursing them or beating them. Now that she was married, she felt it incumbent on her to behave as the mistress of the house, not with the gentle shyness befitting a girl—she must show her authority to keep others under her thumb. (ch. 79)

115. "Sun Shao-tsu cares for nothing but women, gambling and drinking," she [Ying-chun] sobbed. "He's had affairs with practically all our maids and young servants' wives. When I remonstrated mildly two or three times, he cursed me for being jealous, saying I must have been steeped in vinegar. He also says he put five thousand taels in father's safe-keeping and he shouldn't have spent it. He's come here several times to ask for it back, and when he fails to get it he points at me and scolds, 'Don't put on those ladified airs with me! Your old man has spent five thousand taels of mine; so he's sold you to me. If you don't behave yourself, I'll beat you up and send you to sleep with the servants. When your grandfather was alive, seeing how rich and influential our family was, he went to great trouble to get connected with us. Actually, I belong to your father's

generation. It was a mistake my marrying you because that's made me step down one generation, as if I were the one chasing after power and profit.'" (ch. 80)

116. Chia Cheng of course understood his drift.

"Why didn't you tell me earlier?" he repeated.

"I dared not, sir. Now that you ask me, it's my duty to speak; but if I do, most likely you will be angry."

"Not if what you say makes sense."

"Those clerks and runners all bribed their way into this yamen; so of course they all want to feather their nests," Li explained. "They have families to support. Since you came to this post, sir, and before you've achieved anything for the state, there's already been talk."

"What are people saying?"

"The common folk say, 'The stricter the orders a new official gives, the more grasping he will be. The more frightened the county officials, the bigger the bribes they'll send in.'

"When the time comes to levy grain, your yamen officials say they have orders from the new commissioner not to accept any money, and this makes it difficult for those country people who'd rather grease their palms and be done with it. So instead of praising you, sir, they complain that you don't understand the situation. But your close friend and kinsman has climbed to the top in just a few years, simply because he has the good sense to please both his superiors and his inferiors."

"Rubbish," protested Chia Cheng. "Are you implying that I lack sense? As for pleasing both superiors and inferiors, do you want me to connive with rogues—to be 'a cat sleeping with rats'?"

"I spoke frankly, sir, out of concern for you, not wanting to keep anything back," Li answered. "If you were to go on like this till you had no achievements to your credit and your reputation was damaged, you could accuse me of disloyalty for not putting the facts before you."

"What would you do in my place?"

"Just this, sir. While you're in your prime, with friends at court and the old lady in good health, look after your own interests. Otherwise, in less than a year you'll have spent all your family's money and made those above and below resent you too. They'll all assume that in this provincial post Your Lordship must be salting money away. So if some trouble crops up, who's going to help you? By then it will be hard to clear yourself and too late to regret!"

"Are you advising me to become a corrupt official? Forfeiting my life would be of less consequence, but would you have my ancestors deprived of their noble titles?"

"A gentleman of your discernment, sir, must surely have noticed which officials have landed in trouble in recent years. All old friends of Your Lordship's they were, and you often remarked on their probity; but now what has become of their good name? On the other hand, some relatives whom you have always run down have been promoted. It all depends on how well one handles things. You must understand the need, sir, to care for the local officials as well as for the people. Why, if you had your way, sir, and wouldn't let the local magistrates make a cent, who would handle all the work in the provinces? All you need to do is keep up appearances, living up to your good name as an honest official, while in private we underlings get the job done and take whatever blame there may be without involving Your Lordship. We have been so long in your service, sir, you can surely rest assured of our loyalty."

Chia Cheng did not know what rejoinder to make to this.

"I can't risk my life!" he exclaimed. "If you get into trouble. I won't be responsible." He then retired to his room.

After that Li Shih-erh assumed great airs, conniving with others inside and outside the yamen to handle affairs unbeknown to Chia Cheng, who felt so satisfied that all was going smoothly that, far from suspecting Li, he trusted him completely. Certain accusations were brought against his office, but in view of Chia Cheng's austerity and honesty his superiors made no investigations. Only some of his secretaries who were well informed warned him what was happening; and when he did not believe them some resigned while those on good terms with him remained to help out. So the government grain was collected and shipped off without any scandal. (v. 3, ch. 99)

117. He [Chen Pao-yu] talked and talked but said not a word about seeking for truth, just holding forth on scholarship and the management of affairs, as well as loyalty and filial piety. Isn't such a person a toady? (Pao-yu) (ch. 115)

118. The Reverend Void threw back his head and laughed, then tossed him [Tsao Hsueh-chin] the manuscript and left saying to himself, "So it's all hot air—fantastic! Neither author, transcriber, nor readers can tell what it is about. It is nothing but a literary diversion to entertain readers."

When this tale later came to be read, someone wrote four lines of verse to elucidate the author's meaning, as follows:
A tale of grief is told,
Fantasy most melancholy.
Since all live in a dream,
Why laugh at others' folly? (ch. 120)

"Du Shiniang Sinks Her Jewel Box in Anger," comp. Feng Menglong, in *Stories to Caution the World: A Ming Dynasty Collection*, trans. Shuhui Yang and Yunqin Yang, v. 2, U. of Washington Press, 2005

119. The ancients said, "Friendship based on profit falls apart when the money runs out."

120. When Sun Fu came over to try to calm her, Shiniang pushed Li aside and unleashed an explosion of furious words on Sun Fu. "Mr. Li and I went through a lot together before we got here. But you cajoled him with clever words out of lecherous motives and destroyed a marriage of love in one day. You are my worst enemy. If my spirit survives my death, I'll certainly bring a complaint against you to the gods. As for the pleasures of the pillow, you don't have a ghost of a chance!"

Turning to Li Jia, she went on, "In my years as a courtesan, I put away some private savings to support myself in the future. After we met, you and I took many a vow of lifelong love and fidelity. Before we left the capital, I had my sisters give me what were in fact my own possessions. The treasures hidden in the jewel box were worth no less than ten thousand taels of silver. I meant to add some grandeur to your return, so that your parents might act out of compassion and accept me as a member of the family. With the remainder of my life committed to you, I would have had no regrets in life and in death. Little did I know that you trusted me so little that you followed some evil advice and abandoned me before the journey was even completed. You have betrayed my devotion to you. I opened the box and showed its contents in public so that you'll know that a mere thousand taels of silver are of little importance to me. I am not unlike a jewel box that contains precious jade, but you have eyes that fail to recognize value. Alas, I was not born under a lucky star. Having just freed myself from the tribulations of a courtesan's life, I find myself abandoned again. All those present will testify, by the evidence of their eyes and ears, that I have not failed you in any way. It's you who have betrayed me!"

121. In later times, when commenting on the account we have given above, people had this to say: Sun Fu, in scheming to gain a beauty and lightly throwing away a thousand taels of silver, was by no means a decent sort; Li Jia, in failing to appreciate Du Shiniang's devotion, was nothing but an imbecile on whom it was not worth wasting one's breath. But Shiniang was a true heroine of all time. She could very well have found a worthy husband and had a blissful marriage, and yet, she picked Li, whose character she misjudged. As a result, a bright pearl, a piece of fine jade, was thrown in front of a blind man. How tragic that love turned to hate and went into the flowing river!

***Flowers in the Mirror*, Li Ju-chen, trans. and ed. Lin Tai-yi, U. of California Press, 1965 (abr.)**
122. Having finished what they came to do, the maids retreated, and a black-bearded fellow came in with a bolt of white silk. Kneeling down before him, the fellow said, 'I am ordered to bind Your Highness's feet.'

Two other maids seized Lin's feet as the black-bearded one sat down on a low stool, and began to rip the silk into ribbons. Seizing Lin's right foot, he set it upon his knee, and sprinkled white alum powder between the toes and the grooves of the foot. He squeezed the toes tightly together, bent them down so that the whole foot was shaped like an arch, and took a length of white silk and bound it tightly around it twice. One of the others sewed the ribbon together in small stitches. Again the silk went around the foot, and again, it was sewn up.

Merchant Lin felt as though his feet were burning, and wave after wave of pain rose to his heart. When he could stand it no longer, he let out his voice and began to cry. (ch. 13)

123. The woman said to the caning boys, 'Since he is willing, you apply yourselves to the job properly now! If you don't, look out for your lives!'

At this, the caning boys went to work. Two of them held the bandit chief down, while the other two took up big planks, and applied them to the bandit's body. His skin split open and his flesh tore. The bandit screamed. When the twenty strokes had been given, the boys stopped.

'Twenty more!' the woman cried. 'This heartless bandit is not going to get off so easily!'

The bandit chief sobbed, 'Please, Madam! I cannot endure any more!'

'Then why has the idea of taking concubines been on your mind constantly? Would you like it if I took a gigolo, and cast you aside? In times of poverty, you men sometimes know what is right and what is wrong. But when you get rich, you forget not only your old friends and relatives, but even the wife who struggled with you in your hard days! And with your nose up in the air, you think only of yourselves! For that alone you ought to be cut up into ten thousand pieces, and you are still thinking of taking concubines! . . . After today, I will not interfere with you any more. If you don't want to take concubines, all right. If you do, all right, too. But find me a gigolo first. This gigolo, or what the ancients call "Face and Head", will be handsome in the face, and have a full head of hair on his head. And I will not be setting any precedent either, but only following the customs of ancient times.' (ch. 20)

Fortress Besieged, Qian Zhongshu, trans. Jeanne Kelly and Nathan K. Mao, New Directions, 2004

124. Finding himself pressured on both sides, Fang Hung-chien finally realized the importance of a foreign diploma. This diploma, it seemed, would function the same as Adam and Eve's figleaf. It could hide a person's shame and wrap up his disgrace. This tiny square of paper could cover his shallowness, ignorance, and stupidity. Without it, it was as if he were spiritually stark naked and had nothing to bundle up in. But as for getting a degree at that point, whether by studying toward it himself or hiring a ghost writer to write a dissertation, there was neither time nor money. A Ph.D. from the nearby University of Hamburg was considered the easiest to muddle through, but even it required six months. He could just go ahead and deceive his family by saying he'd received a Ph.D., but then he was afraid that he couldn't fool his father and father-in-law. (ch. 1)

125. Mr. Chang was used to dealing with foreigners and his speech had a special characteristic—perhaps in a foreign firm, the YMCA, the Rotary Club, or other such places, this was nothing unusual—he liked to sprinkle his Chinese with meaningless English expressions. It wasn't that he had new ideas, which were difficult to express in Chinese and required the use of English. The English words inlaid in his speech could not thus be compared with the gold teeth inlaid in one's mouth, since gold teeth are not only decorative but functional as well. A better comparison would be with the bits of meat stuck between the teeth—they show that one has had a good meal but are otherwise useless. He imitated the American accent down to the slightest inflection, though maybe the nasal sound was a little overdone, sounding more like a Chinese with a cold and a stuffy nose, rather than an American speaking. The way he said "Very well" sounded just like a dog growling—"*Vurry wul.*" A pity the Romans never had a chance to hear it, for otherwise the Latin poet Persius would not have been the only one to say that "r" was a nasal in the dog's alphabet (*sonat hic de nare canina litera*). (ch. 2)

126. You are right, Miss T'ang. At the Chous where I live, there's a phone right outside my room. The noise gives me a headache every day. Often at the most unreasonable hours, such as in the middle of the night or in early morning, someone will call. It's such a nuisance. Luckily televiewing isn't in wide use; otherwise it'd be even worse. There'd be people spying on you when you're in the bathtub or in bed. As education becomes increasingly widespread, the number of people writing letters decreases. (Hung-chien) (ch. 3)

127. Hung-chien said, "That's not a great professor engaging in politics. It's a petty politician running education. The former policy of keeping the masses ignorant prevented the people from getting an education. The current policy of keeping the masses ignorant only allows the people to get a certain kind of education. The uneducated are fooled by others because they're illiterate. The educated are taken in by printed matter like your newspaper propaganda and lecture notes on training cadres because they are literate." (ch. 4)

128. Having so much leisure time of late, Tun-weng had suddenly discovered himself, like a child who is fascinated with his image in the mirror as he moves his head from side to side, and gazes at himself from the corner of his eye. This spiritual narcissism had prompted him to write an autobiography and keep a diary. It was like a woman who puts on Chinese and Western dresses of all seasons and all colors, strikes every kind of pose, walking, standing, sitting, lying, supporting chin in hand and twisting the neck, and has a picture taken of each to give her friends as a memento.

These records were to prove from every angle and with every kind of fact Fang Tun-weng's noble character. Now whenever he said or did something, he was thinking at the same time how to record it in his diary or his record of deeds and sayings. The records weren't completely concocted out of thin air and were like a water bubble, which leaves a tiny drop of water when it bursts. Students of the psychology of language will recognize this at once as a case of *verbalmania:* People with a desire to lead, no matter whether in the literary, military, commercial, or governmental field, all reveal this symptom. (ibid.)

129. Roasted sweet potatoes are like illicit sex in the old Chinese saying, "Having it isn't as good as not having it." The smell is better than the taste. When you smell it, you feel you must have one, but once you actually sink your teeth into it, you find it's not really anything special. (ch. 5)

130. "Why don't ghosts grow up?" asked Miss Sun innocently. "Children who've been dead for decades are still children."

     Hung-chien replied, "That's why separation or death is preferred to 'spending a lifetime together.' It can keep people from aging. Not only do ghosts not grow old, but friends we haven't seen for a long time remain just as dashing in our mind's eye as they were then, even though we ourselves have already grown old." (ibid.)

131. Of course, this added a new uneasiness, but this kind of uneasiness was out in the open and exposed to the sunlight, not like the business of the bought diploma, every trace of which, like a corpse in a murder case, had to be hidden even from himself. The only way to lie and deceive was as Han Hsüeh-yü had done it. One had to have the courage to carry it all the way through. He was just no good at it. What a big fool—to have lied and still tried to maintain his honesty. If he had just gone boldly and brazenly ahead, he could at least have avoided Kao Sung-nien's bullying. (ch. 6)

132. Hsin-mei said, "Maybe I was too young and inexperienced then to judge him correctly. But I think Kao Sung-nien has come up in the world these last few years. When a person gets in a high position, he's apt to get carried away." He didn't realize that a person's shortcomings are just like a monkey's tail. When it's squatting on the ground, its tail is hidden from view, but as soon as it climbs a tree, it exposes its backside to everyone. Nevertheless, the long tail and red bottom were there all the time. They aren't just a mark of having climbed to a higher position. (ibid.)

133. Hsin-mei and Hung-chien had not only become quite used to hearing this sort of talk lately; they had even gotten in the habit of saying it themselves. To be sure, the ravages of the war had left many people with wealth and property homeless and destitute, but at the same time it gave an untold number of the destitute an opportunity to hark back to their days as millionaires. The Japanese had burned so many nonexistent houses with towers in the sky, taken possession of so many nonexistent properties, and destroyed so many one-sided romances made in heaven! (ch. 7)

134. Just as getting a degree is a matter of duping one's professors with a thesis, so teaching is a matter of duping the students with the lecture material. Hung-chien had not duped his professors, and so he had not received his degree. Now that he wanted to dupe his students, he found he lacked a model to go by. There are two stages a professor must go through to become a star professor. First, he must make his lecture notes into a book, and second, he must use the book as his lectures.

It is much like an apprentice barber who sharpens his skills by practicing on the heads of idiots or poor people. Thus, if a professor's lectures went off smoothly when tried out in the classroom, they could be published in a book. After publication, it would of course become a required text-book. Since Hung-chien was putting so much effort into his teaching, it was only natural that he should begin to have wild dreams of glory. (ibid.)

135. Hsin-mei said, ". . . For students, social gatherings provide a chance for men and women to meet. When I was in America, people used to call the Foreign Students Summer Club the 'Big Three Conference': the show-offs, the suckers, and the—uh—the girl-snowers."

They all laughed. Mrs. Chao laughed till she began to cough and forbade Hsin-mei to utter any more nonsense. Wen-wan laughed more tersely than the rest and said, "You were in the Summer Club yourself. Don't deny it. I saw that picture. Which of the Big Three were you?"

Hsin-mei was unable to answer. (ch. 8)

136. You, you little fool, are the only one who can't get her out of your mind! I've long since forgotten her. She's probably married, become a mother, and doesn't even remember me any more. Now when I think how serious I used to be about love before I got married, it really seems naïve. The fact is, no matter whom you marry, after you're married, you'll find it's not the same person but someone else. If people knew that before marriage they could skip all that stuff about courtship, romance, and so on. When two people get to know each other and fall in love, they both conceal their true faces so that the whole time up until they get married they still don't know each other. It's the old-fashioned marriages that are more straightforward. Neither party gets to know the other before marriage. (Hung-chien) (ch. 9)

Frog, Mo Yan, trans. Howard Goldblatt, Viking, 2015
137. In 1953, villagers were adamantly opposed to new midwifery methods, thanks to rumours spread by old midwives, who said that children born through these methods were prone to be arthritic. Why would they spread such rumours? Because once the new methods caught on, they'd be out of work. Delivering a baby at the mother's home meant a free meal, a pair of towels, and a dozen eggs. Whenever these women entered the conversation, my aunt – Gugu – ground her teeth in anger. She could not begin to calculate how many infants and pregnant women had died at those old witches' hands. Her descriptions of their methods were chilling: they grew long fingernails, their eyes emitted green will-o'-the-wisp-like glimmers, and their breath stank. She said they pressed down on the mother's belly with rolling pins and stuffed rags in their mouths to keep the foetuses from coming out there. They knew nothing about anatomy and were totally ignorant of a woman's biological make-up. When they encountered a difficult birth, according to Gugu, they crammed their hands up the birth canal and pulled with all their might, sometimes actually wrenching the womb out along with the foetus. For the longest time, if I'd been asked to compile a list of people most deserving to be lined up and shot, I'd unhesitatingly say: the old midwives. Gradually I came to understand why Gugu was so prejudiced against them. Crude, ignorant old midwives certainly did exist, but experienced old midwives who, through their own experience, had a keen grasp of the secrets of a woman's body, existed as well. (bk. 1, ch. 2)

138. Tell me why I've bumped into scoundrels like that all my life. Then there's that bastard Xiao Shangchun, who damn near killed me during the Cultural Revolution, and now struts around like

a lord and master, waving his palm-leaf fan as he enjoys the good life at home. I hear his son has tested into college. Is that right? What happened to the old saying that 'good is rewarded with good, evil with evil'? The good people suffer, the rotten eggs live like kings, that's what. People still get what's coming to them, Mother said. It just takes time. How much time? Gugu asked her. My hair has already turned white! (bk. 2, ch. 1)

139. Mother said it was common in old times for a woman and her mother-in-law to have children at the same time. Now? It could still happen. A girl in my daughter's college class has a newborn baby sister. Her father, a coalmine owner who hires migrant workers under slave-like conditions, was immeasurably wealthy. People like that live in luxurious villas in Beijing, Shanghai, Los Angeles, San Francisco, Melbourne and Toronto with their mistresses, who produce babies for them. (bk. 4, ch. 1)

140. No one as bad as Melon Huang deserved to have an heir, and what a shame it was that Wang Xiaomei was carrying his child. I'd learned enough from delivering all those children to know that a person's core—good or bad—is determined more by nature than nurture. You can criticise hereditary laws all you want, but this is knowledge based on experience. You could place a son of that evil Melon Huang in a Buddhist temple, and he'd grow up to be a lascivious monk. (Gugu) (ch. 4)

141. Sensei, I wrapped my arms around my head and crouched down out of feelings of despair. . . . It was at a restaurant called Wild Pheasant on a street near the People's Playhouse. As we walked up to read a poster in front of the playhouse we tripped over a metal chain connected to a red and white post, which fell to the ground, not even close to the rear of a white car parked there. But a young woman with hair dyed a golden yellow, a pinched face, and lips as thin as knife blades, who was sitting in front of Wild Pheasant, ran over to the car, spotted a white ding on it and accused us of causing it. With wild gestures, she tore into us verbally, using all sorts of Beijing gutter talk. She said she'd lived her whole life in that lane and had seen every kind of person there was. But what do you out-of-town turtles climb out of your burrows and come to the capital to do? Embarrass the Chinese people? Fat, and reeking of haemorrhoid cream, she charged me, fists swinging, and bloodied my nose. Young men with shaved heads and bare-chested old men stood by shouting encouragement and showing off as old-time Beijingers, insisting that we apologise and make restitution. Sensei, weak as always, I gave her the money and said I was sorry. When we got home, Sensei, we wept first and then decided to move back to Northeast Gaomi Township. Since this was our hometown, I didn't think I'd have to worry about being bullied here. But these two women were every bit as vicious as the woman on Snack Street in Beijing. What I don't understand, Sensei, is why people have to be so horrible. (ch. 10)

"The Golden Cangue," Eileen Chang, trans. the author, in *Modern Chinese Stories and Novellas 1919–1949*, ed. Joseph S. M. Lau, C. T. Hsia, and Leo Ou-fan Lee, Columbia UP, 1981

142. On the bed lay her husband, that lifeless body . . .

   Some people tried to make matches for her. If the other side was not well off, Ch'i-ch'iao would always suspect it wanted their money. If the other side had wealth and influence, it would show little enthusiasm. Ch'ang-an had only average good looks, and since her mother was not only lowborn but also known for her shrewishness, she probably would not have much upbringing. So the high were out of reach and the low Ch'i-ch'iao would not stoop to—Ch'ang-an stayed home year after year.

Life is so devious and unreasonable. Why had she married into the Chiang family? For money? No, to meet Chi-tse, because it was fated that she should be in love with him. She lifted her face slightly. He was standing in front of her with flat hands closed on her fan and his cheek pressed against it. He was ten years older too, but, he was after all the same person. Could he be lying to her? He wanted her money—the money she had sold her life for? The very idea enraged her. Even if she had him wrong there, could he have suffered as much for her as she did for him? Now that she had finally given up all thoughts of love he was here again to tempt her. His eyes—after ten years he was still the same person. Even if he were lying to her, wouldn't it be better to find out a little later? Even if she knew very well it was lies, he was such a good actor, wouldn't it be almost real?

***The Grand Scribe's Records*, Ssu-ma Ch'ien, v. 7, *The Memoirs of Pre-Han China*, ed. William H. Nienhauser, Jr., trans. Tsai-fa Cheng, et al., Indiana UP, 1994**

143. His Honor the Grand Scribe says: ". . . Some say, 'Heaven's way favors none, but always sides with good men.' Can men such as Po Yi and Shu Ch'i be called good then, or bad? They accumulated such virtue, kept their actions this pure, and died of starvation.

"Of his seventy disciples, Confucius recommended only Yen Yüan as 'fond of learning.' But 'Hui [Yen Yüan] was often poor,' and did not get his fill of even rice dregs and husks, finally dying young. How then does Heaven repay good men?

"The Bandit Chih killed innocent men daily, made delicacies from men's flesh, was cruel and ruthless, willful and arrogant, gathered a band of thousands of men and wreaked havoc across the world, yet finally died of old age. From what virtue did this follow?

"These are just the most notorious and best known examples. As for more recent times, men who do not follow what is proper in their actions, and do nothing but violate taboos are still carefree and happy for all their lives and wealthy for generations without end; men who choose carefully how they tread, wait for the right time to offer their words, in walking do not take shortcuts, and except for what is right and fair do not vent pent-up emotions, still encounter disaster and catastrophe in numbers beyond counting. I am deeply perplexed by all this. Perhaps this is what is meant by 'the Way of Heaven.' Is it? Or isn't it?" ("Po Yi, Memoir 1," 4)

144. Tsai Yü fell asleep in the daytime. The master said, "Rotten wood cannot be carved and a wall of dirty mud cannot be trowelled." ("Confucius's Disciples, Memoir 7," 69)

***The Grand Scribe's Records*, Ssu-ma Ch'ien, v. 9, *The Memoirs of Han China*, pt. 2, ed. William H, Nienhauser, Jr., trans. J. Michael Farmer, et al., Indiana UP, 2011**

145. That which brings ill to people, is that illnesses are numerous, but that which brings ill to physicians, is that the ways to treat illnesses are few. Therefore, in illnesses, there are six [types of people] that are not treatable: arrogant and reckless people who cannot be reasoned with are the first that cannot be treated; those who do not consider their physical bodies important, but emphasize wealth are the second that cannot be treated; those who are not able to dress and eat appropriately are the third who cannot be treated. Those whose *yin* and *yang* join and whose visceral *ch'i* is unstable are the fourth who cannot be treated. Those whose bodily form is thin and weak and cannot take medicine are the fifth who cannot be treated. Those who believe in shamans

but do not believe in physicians are the sixth who cannot be treated. If one has one of these [types], then they are extremely hard to treat. ("Pien Ch'üeh and Ts'ang-kung, Memoir 45," "P'ien Ch'üeh," trans. William H. Nienhauser, Jr., Indiana, 16)

146. His Honor the Grand Scribe says: ["]When Chu-fu Yen was on the road [to power], all the ministers praised him, [but] when his name was ruined and he himself put to death, gentlemen competed with each other to speak of his wickedness. How sad![("] (389)

The Grand Scribe's Records, Ssu-ma Ch'ien, v. 10, The Memoirs of Han China, pt. 3, ed. William H. Nienhauser, Jr., trans. Chiu Ming Chan, et al., Indiana UP, 2016
147. His Honor the Grand Scribe said: "Take the worthiness of Chi [An] and Cheng [Tang-shih], [when they] held positions of power, then the guests and retainers [increased] ten-fold, [when they] did not hold positions of power, then it was not like this; how much more so would it be for a man of the masses? Of Honorable Chai from Hsia-kuei it is said: 'In the beginning, when Honorable Chai served as Commandant of Justice, the guests and retainers filled his gate. When he was dismissed, outside of his gate one could set up bird nets. When he became Commandant of Justice once more, the guests and retainers wished to flock to him [again]. Only then did Honorable Chai inscribe upon his gate in bold letters: "Once dead, once alive, only then does one know one's friends' affection. Once poor, once rich, only then does one know one's friends' attitude. Once ennobled, once disdained, one's friends' affection can only then be seen."' [These words] can also be said of Chi [An] and Cheng [Tang-shih], how sad!" (259–60)

The Great Thoughts of China: 3,000 Years of Wisdom that Shaped a Civilization, Liang Cong-jie, ed. Todd Lappin, John Wiley & Sons, 1996
148. People often say they can be content with poverty and humble station. In reality they are merely helpless and know of no way out, and their ability is too small for them to do anything. If they could make any move, they would not remain content. Only when one truly realizes that moral principles are more enjoyable than achievement of wealth or the fulfillment of material desires can he remain content. (Zhang Zai, 8)

149. In later generations, from the common people to the great lords, people turn their minds to glory and honor every day. Farmers, artisans, and merchants turn their minds to wealth and extravagance every day. Millions and millions of people, each with his own mind, compete for wealth. The world is thus in great confusion. How can there be unity? It is hard to see how the world can fail to become chaotic. (Cheng Yi, 51)

Han Ying da ci dian = Chinese-English Dictionary, editor in chief, Wu Guanghua, Shanghai Jiaotong UP, 1997
150. Each one sweeps the snow from his own doorstep and does not bother about the frost on his neighbour's roof. (909)

151. A beautiful girl has (often) an unfortunate life. (1098)

152. You can change mountains and rivers but not a person's nature. (1295)

153. Extreme joy begets sorrow. (1539)

154. Where ignorance is bliss, it's folly to be wise. (v. 2, 1820)

155. Clasp Buddha's feet when in dire need, but refuse to burn incense when all is well. (1939)

156. Shoot the bird which takes the lead. (2013)

157. Heaven destroys those who don't look out for themselves (motto of an egoist). (2120)

158. A man dreads fame as a pig dreads being fat. (2126)

159. Human beings die in pursuit of wealth, and birds die in pursuit of food. (2129)

160. When those above behave unworthily, those below will do the same. (2220)

161. Puff oneself up at one's own cost. (2411)

162. If you have money, you can make the devil push the millstone for you. (3106)

***Han Ying Zhongguo wen hua ci dian (A Chinese-English Dictionary of Chinese Culture)*, editor in chief, Simade School, trans. Cao Jianxin, Nanjing UP, 2005**
163. Say every fine word and do every foul deed. (135)

164. Good news never goes beyond the gate, while bad news spreads far and wide. (136)

165. Be fond of eating and averse to work. (136)

166. A man who rests content with nothing is like a snake trying to swallow an elephant. (ibid.)

167. The magistrates are free to burn down houses, while the common people are forbidden even to light lamps. (495)

***The HarperCollins World Reader*, [ed.] Mary Ann Caws, Christopher Prendergast, single vol. ed., HarperCollins, 1994**
168. Li Chi pleaded again and again: "It is the truth that I bought it from an old cooper. I know nothing about a murder. How would I dare to make a false statement?"

"This old man you bought it from," went on the interrogating officer, "what was his name and where did he come from? Give me the true facts and I will have him brought in. Then we shall get at the truth, and you will be released."

"I simply bought it from him when I ran into him on the street," said Li Chi. "I really don't know what his name is or where he lives."

The interrogating officer began to abuse him: "You're only trying to confuse the issue. Are you hoping to make someone else pay for this man's life? We must go by the concrete evidence, this canary. This rascal won't confess, until he's beaten."

Li Chi was flogged over and over until the flesh was ripped open. He could not bear the pain, and had no alternative but to make up a story that when he saw what a fine bird this canary was he had killed Shen Hsiu and cast his head away. Thereupon Li Chi was committed to the main jail, while the officer of the Grand Court prepared his report for submission to the Emperor. The Imperial rescript ran: "Li Chi was beyond doubt the murderer of Shen Hsiu, the canary being the evidence of this. The law requires that he shall be executed." (Anonymous, *Stories Ancient and Modern [Ku-chin-hsiao-shuo]*, "The Canary Murders," trans. Cyril Birch, 1464)

169. The out-of-the-way county in this story has been designated by the Taiwan provincial government as a developing area. Its urban center is a small town of forty or fifty thousand people. When the town youth are in the presence of people from the outlying countryside, they habitually put on airs of self-importance to show that they are urbanites; the somewhat older people, with their greater understanding of humility, will go no further than to nod their heads with slightly superior smiles on their faces. People from the countryside cheerfully and loudly tell anyone within earshot stories of their daughters who have married men from town. And even though the ears of the listeners ring with this barrage of talk, they feel it only proper, for were they to have an eligible young daughter, she too would leave the farm and marry a townsman (so they think). Even greater glory comes to someone whose son brings a townswoman back to the farm as his wife, for no matter how their lives together turn out in the end, at least in the beginning there is a great deal of loud, enthusiastic talk. (Huang Ch'un-ming [Huang Chunming], "The Drowning of an Old Cat," trans. Howard Goldblatt, 1490–91)

"The Herbivorous Family," Mo Yan, in Shelley W. Chan, *A Subversive Voice in China: The Fictional World of Mo Yan*, Cambria, 2011
170. Hey, humans, don't have too high an opinion of yourselves, don't give yourselves the air of being the wisest of all species. Essentially human beings are no different from dogs, cats, maggots in manure buckets, or bugs in wall cracks. What best distinguishes humankind from animals is: humans are hypocritical! . . . What creatures are humans? When a wolf eats a lamb, it is condemned by humanity as fierce and cruel. Human beings, however, after enjoying a delicious dish of mutton, they belch and tell innocent kids the story of the beautiful and meek lamb. What kind of creature is a human? (205)

***The Huainanzi: A Guide to the Theory and Practice of Government in Early Han China*, Liu An, King of Huainan, trans. John S. Major, et al., Columbia UP, 2010**
171. If not for small learning, a person would not be greatly misled;
if not for small intelligence, a person would not be greatly deluded. ("A Mountain of Persuasions," 16.2, 626)

172. All people diligently make preparations in case of disaster, yet none is able to understand how to prevent a disaster from occurring. Preventing a disaster is easier than preparing for a disaster, yet none apply themselves to this task, so there is not yet anyone with whom to discuss this art. (18.18, 741)

173. Humaneness is what the common people admire;
    Rightness is what the masses exalt.
    To do what people admire,
    to practice what people exalt:

this is what the stern father teaches his sons,

and the way in which the loyal minister serves his ruler.

However, in any age there are those who use them and [suffer] personal death and the loss of their states, because they do not understand the times. (18.23, 747)

174. Shan Bao turned away from the age and departed from the vulgar. He lived on a cliff and drank from a valley [stream]. He did not wear silk or hemp; he did not eat the five grains. After seventy years he still had the complexion of a child. In the end he met a hungry tiger who killed and ate him.

Zhang Yi was fond of courtesy.

Whenever he crossed the palace court, he always hurried;

Whenever he encountered anyone from his village he always bowed.

He treated all servants and grooms with the utmost propriety. But he did not live out his life span; he developed a fever and died.

Bao nurtured his interior, and a tiger ate his exterior;

Yi cultivated his exterior, and sickness attacked his interior. (18.24, 749)

175. What makes it difficult to understand affairs is that [people] hide their origins and conceal their tracks; they establish the selfish in the place of the impartial; they incline toward the deviant over the correct and confuse other people's minds with victory. (18.27, 755)

176. The weakness of a wise person [in some field] makes him not as good [in that field] as a foolish person who is strong [in it].

The deficits of a worthy [in some field] make him not as good [in that field] as an ordinary person who surpasses [in it]. ("Cultivating Effort," 19.5, 777)

177. People who follow the conventions of the present age mostly revere the ancient and scorn the present. Thus those who formulate [teachings of] the Way necessarily ascribe them to the Divine Farmer or the Yellow Emperor; only then will they proceed with their discussion. Muddled rulers of chaotic eras venerate what is remote and what proceeds therefrom, so they value such things. Those who study are blinded by their theories and respect [only] what they have heard. (19.7, 783)

178. A music master from Handan made up a new tune and said it was composed by Li Qi. All the people vied to learn it. Later when they discovered it was not written by Li Qi, they all abandoned the tune. This was a case of not even beginning to know about music.

A country fellow found a rough piece of jade. Being pleased by its appearance, he considered it to be precious and hid it away. When he showed it to others, people considered that it was just a stone, so he threw it away. This was a case of not even beginning to know about jade. (784)

179. Nowadays a person of average talent, benighted by ignorant and deluded wisdom, cloaked in insulting and shameful conduct, who has no training in his own calling or in the techniques that are his responsibility—how could he not make people look askance at him and hold their noses? (787)

***I Love Dollars and Other Stories of China*, Zhu Wen, trans. Julia Lovell, Columbia UP, 2007**

180. But the next generation, my generation, is different: greedy for everything, everywhere, smashing, grabbing, swearing. Because they write for money, for women, everyone thinks they're going places. But it's exhausting, this life of theirs; not all of them can stay the course, they get kidney problems, they get beyond medical help. Drink up, Dad, I've told you all there is to know about me. ("I Love Dollars")

181. Practically ever since they emerged from the primordial swamp, humans have had four choices in how to get from A to B: first, walk or climb; second, swim, the precondition for which is knowing how to swim; third, fly, for which you need to grab hold of an ample bird to whom you have clearly explained your desired destination. The final option—rolling—has proved the most popular across the centuries and millennia. Now, this last mode of travel comes in motorized and nonmotorized forms, the former dividing into further subcategories according to size and power of engine. Nonmotorized modes of wheeled transport come in two varieties, animal- and human-powered, easily distinguished by a respective tendency, or lack thereof, to defecate in public. But all types of rolling have one point in common: every single one effects spatial motion through the agency of wheels. The crucial historical shift, the force driving humanity ever forward, ever faster toward meltdown, is the move from two legs to the wheel. At this advanced hour in history, even I, a mere boiler serviceman in an electrical factory, can sense that we're freewheeling helplessly, inexorably toward some kind of doomsday. ("Wheels")

***The Importance of Living*, Lin Yutang, Morrow, 1998**

182. There is a wealth of humbug in this life, but the multitudinous little humbugs have been classified by Chinese Buddhists under two big humbugs: fame and wealth. There is a story that Emperor Ch'ienlung once went up a hill overlooking the sea during his trip to South China and saw a great number of sailing ships busily plying the China Sea to and fro. He asked his minister what the people in those hundreds of ships were doing, and his minister replied that he saw only two ships, and their names were "Fame" and "Wealth." Many cultured persons were able to escape the lure of wealth, but only the very greatest could escape the lure of fame. Once a monk was discoursing with his pupil on these two sources of worldly cares, and said: "It is easier to get rid of the desire for money than to get rid of the desire for fame. Even retired scholars and monks still want to be distinguished and well-known among their company. They want to give public discourses to a large audience, and not retire to a small monastery talking to one pupil, like you and me now." The pupil replied: "Indeed, Master, you are the only man in the world who has conquered the desire for fame!" And the Master smiled.

From my own observation of life, this Buddhist classification of life's humbugs is not complete, and the great humbugs of life are three, instead of two: Fame, Wealth and Power. There is a convenient American word which again combines these three humbugs into the One Great Humbug: Success. But many wise men know that the desires for success, fame and wealth are euphemistic names for the fears of failure, poverty and obscurity, and that these fears dominate our lives. (101–02)

183. Nothing shows more conclusively a small mind than a little government bureaucrat suffering from illusions of his own grandeur, or a social upstart displaying her jewels, or a half-baked writer imagining himself to belong to the company of the immortals and immediately becoming a less simple and less natural human being. (103–04)

184. It is against the will of God to eat delicate food hastily, to pass gorgeous views hurriedly, to express deep sentiments superficially, to pass a beautiful day steeped in food and drinks, and to enjoy your wealth steeped in luxuries. (328)

***Literatures of Asia: From Antiquity to the Present*, ed. Tony Barnstone, Prentice Hall, 2003**
185. The ancient saints and sages are forgotten.
Only the fame of great drunks
goes from generation to generation. (Li Bai, "Song on Bringing in the Wine," trans. Willis Barnstone, Tony Barnstone, and Chou Ping, 257)

186. A show of arrogant spirit fills the road;
a glitter of saddles and horses lights up the dust.
I ask who these people are—
Trusted servants of the ruler, I'm told.
The vermilion sashes are all high-ranking courtiers;
the purple ribbons are probably generals.
Proudly they repair to the regimental feast,
their galloping horses passing like clouds.
Tankards and wine cups brim with nine kinds of spirits;
from water and land, an array of eight delicacies.
For fruit they break open Tung-t'ing oranges,
for fish salad, carve up scaly bounty from T'ien-ch'ih.
Stuffed with food, they rest content in heart;
livened by wine, their mood grows merrier than ever.
This year there's a drought south of the Yangtze.
In Ch'ü-chou, people are eating people. (Bo [Bai] Juyi (Po Chü-i), "Light Furs, Fat Horses," trans. Burton Watson, 290)

187. Alas, who knew that the land rent and taxes could be even more poisonous than a snake? (Liu Zongyuan (Liu Tsung-yüan), "The Snake-Catcher," 293)

188. During the reign of Xuan De, cricket fights were popular at court and a levy of crickets was exacted every year. Now these crickets were scarce in the province of Shaanxi, but the magistrate of Huayin—to get into the good books of the governor—presented a cricket which proved a remarkable fighter. So much so that his county was commanded to present crickets regularly and the magistrate ordered his bailiffs to produce them. The young fellows in town began to keep crickets and demand high prices for them, while the crafty bailiffs seized this chance to make money. Thus each cricket they collected was the ruin of several households. (Pu Songling (Pu Sung-ling), "Cricket," trans. Yang Xianyi and Gladys Yang, 358)

189. No matter how you looked at it, writing and criticism were just two forms of pedantry. All the flattery and hostility which were so much a part of the literary life amounted to little more than a waste of paper and ink, and no one engaged in these activities would ever contribute a single new page to human history.

The history of literature and literary criticism was little more than the history of numerous individuals flattering themselves; if these subjects never existed, libraries would certainly be a lot less empty and dull. (Lao She, "Filling a Prescription," trans. Don J. Cohn, 396–97)

190. "What exactly is this new-style proletarian wedding?" Mu Ming asked, trying to look and sound as much like a Red Guard as possible.

"The ceremony will be as follows. First, all present will recite from the Quotations, in particular the Three Speeches. Second, you will invite the leaders of the province, county, and commune to give speeches. Finally, the young couple will bow three times to the portrait of Chairman Mao, once to the assembled leaders, and once to each other. That's it. Of course, there will be no dowry from either family. However, both sides may exchange copies of the Red Book, portraits of our esteemed Chairman, sickles, and manure forks. No entertainment is allowed. After the wedding, the groom will spend the wedding night watering crops, and the bride will make forty posters of the Chairman's Quotations, done in red and yellow paint on wooden boards." (Wang Meng, "Anecdotes of Minister Maimaiti: A Uygur Man's Black Humor," trans. Qingyun Wu, 404)

191. Just think, twelve piglets—Mammy Guo really knows what she's doing. He asked her about her past farm experience and her suggestions for the future.

"I just feed them—that's all. I can't read a single word; don't ask me about my experience," Mammy Guo said, quite pleased with herself.

Yes, what could she say? I have to make up my own report. H'mm—"To carry out the System of Accountability—if every member in the Commune shares the responsibility, the cadre can be assured of success,"—pretty good—but one sentence is not enough—this wine is not bad, must be at least sixty-five per cent alcohol, better than the one I bought last time—Mammy Guo is quite a capable woman, how she mobilizes everybody, old and young, the eighty-year-old father and the school-aged daughter—isn't this an "experience"? "Enlist all help, regardless of age or sex, in our care for the piglets"—sounds nice, but wait, how stupid can I get? This jingle is from the late fifties, no longer popular now. "Mass mobilization means massive achievement"—no good, you don't see such slogans on newspapers anymore. I have to use new expressions, such as "United in heart and spirit, we strive for the Four Modernizations"—that's better—one hears it broadcast eight times a day—but what category of modernization does Mammy Guo's work fit in?—I'd better stop drinking. Tomorrow I have to report to my superior—but what shall I say about "experience"? Pooh—never mind, when the time comes, I'll make up words to suit whatever tune the authority picks. (Chen Rong (Ch'en Jung), "Regarding the Problem of Newborn Piglets in Winter," trans. Chun-ye Shih, 422)

A Little Primer of Tu Fu, David Hawkes, Chinese U. of Hong Kong Press/New York Review Books, 2016

192. They're always mobilizing now! There are some of us who went north at fifteen to garrison the River and who are still, at forty, being sent to the Military Settlements in the west. When we left as lads, the village headman had to tie our headcloths for us. We came back white-haired, but still we have to go back for frontier duty! On those frontier posts enough blood has flowed to fill the sea; but the Martial Emperor's dreams of expansion remain unsatisfied. Haven't you heard, sir, in our land of Han, throughout the two hundred prefectures east of the mountains briers and brambles are growing in thousands of little hamlets; and though many a sturdy wife turns her own hand to the hoeing and ploughing, the crops grow just anywhere, and you can't see where one field ends and the next begins? And it's even worse for the men from Ch'in. Because they make such

good fighters, they are driven about this way and that like so many dogs or chickens. (the conscripts) ("Ballad of the Army Carts," 19)

193. The way of the world is to hate what has had its day; and fortune is as fickle as a lamp-flame. Her husband is not faithful to her. His new woman is as lovely as a jewel. Even the vetch-tree knows when it is evening; and the mandarin ducks do not sleep alone. Yet he has eyes only for the smiles of the new woman: no ear for the sobbing of the old. In the mountain the waters of the stream are clear, but once they have left the mountain they are muddy. ("A Fine Lady," 92–93)

"A Madman's Diary," Lu Hsun, in *Selected Stories of Lu Hsun*, [trans. Yang Hsien-yi and Gladys Yang,] Norton, 2003

194. Everything requires careful consideration if one is to understand it. In ancient times, as I recollect, people often ate human beings, but I am rather hazy about it. I tried to look this up, but my history has no chronology, and scrawled all over each page are the words, "Virtue and Morality." Since I could not sleep anyway, I read intently half the night, until I began to see words between the lines, the whole book being filled with the two words—"Eat people."

***A Manual of Chinese Quotations: Being a Translation of the Ch'êng Yü K'ao*, J. H. Stewart Lockhart, Kelly & Walsh, 1893**

195. He who covets and loves wealth is called "a money fool." (350)

196. He who is fond of purchasing land and houses is called "a land maniac." (ibid.)

197. Wei Chuang counted the grains of rice and then cooked them; and weighed the firewood before lighting it—his parsimony was contemptible. (355)

198. Looking at a leopard through a quill—what one sees is not much (for you only see one spot). (398)

199. Li I-fu, under the cover of mildness, injured (men and) things, so it was said of him "that under his smile was hidden a sword." (403)

200. The Emperor Chung Tsung personally kept count for the Empress Wei (when playing chess with Wu San-ssŭ)—the disgrace of which will spread for thousands of years. (Chung Tsung (A.D. 684), of the T'ang dynasty, was poisoned by the Empress Wei, notorious for her disgraceful intrigues with Wu San-ssŭ.) (406)

***Mencius*, Mencius, trans. D. C. Lau, Penguin, 1970**

201. Mencius said, "The trouble with people is that they are too eager to assume the role of teacher." (IV.A.23)

202. Mencius said, "Slight is the difference between man and the brutes. The common man loses this distinguishing feature, while the gentleman retains it." (IV.B.19)

203. Mencius said, "In good years the young men are mostly lazy, while in bad years they are mostly violent. Heaven has not sent down men whose endowment differs so greatly. The difference is due to what ensnares their hearts." (VI.A.7)

204. In the *Spring and Autumn Annals* there were no just wars. There were only cases of one war not being quite as bad as another. A punitive expedition is a war waged by one in authority against his subordinates. It is not for peers to punish one another by war. (VII.B.2)

205. Mencius said, "A man who is out to make a name for himself will be able to give away a state of a thousand chariots, but reluctance would be written all over his face if he had to give away a basketful of rice and a bowlful of soup when no such purpose was served." (VII.B.11)

206. Mencius said, ". . . The trouble with people is that they leave their own fields to weed the fields of others. They are exacting towards others but indulgent towards themselves." (VII.B.32)

207. "If a man is praised for his honesty in his village," said Wan Tzu, "then he is an honest man wherever he goes. Why did Confucius consider such a man an enemy of virtue?"

If you want to censure him, you cannot find anything; if you want to find fault with him, you cannot find anything either. He shares with others the practices of the day and is in harmony with the sordid world. He pursues such a policy and appears to be conscientious and faithful, and to show integrity in his conduct. He is liked by the multitude and is self-righteous. It is impossible to embark on the way of Yao and Shun with such a man. Hence the name "enemy of virtue" [answered Mencius]. (VII.B.37)

A New Account of Tales of the World = Shih-shuo Hsin-yü, 2nd ed., Liu I-ch'ing, trans. Richard B. Mather, Center for Chinese Studies, U. of Michigan, 2002
208. On the distinctions among the "Three Vehicles" (*san-sheng*) the Buddhists are confused in their interpretations, but Chih Tun's division and definition made all three brilliantly distinct. Listeners sitting below in the lecture hall all said they could explain them, but after Chih had descended from the platform and sat down and they discussed it together among themselves, it appeared they could barely get through the first two. When they entered the third they became confused.

Even today, though Chih Tun's disciples have transmitted his interpretation, they still do not entirely comprehend it. (ch. 4, 118)

209. Hsieh An originally had the determination to live as a recluse in the Eastern Mountains. But later stringent orders from the court kept coming, and, unable any longer to protect himself, he finally went to take up his post as Huan Wen's sergeant-at-arms (in 360). At the time someone made Huan a present of some medicinal herbs, among which was some *yüan-chih* ("far-reaching determination"). Huan took some and asked Hsieh, "This medicine is also called *hsiao-ts'ao* ("small grass"). How is it that the same thing has two names?"

Hsieh did not have time to answer before Hao Lung, who was present at the time, answered in a flash, "That's easy to explain. When you're living as a recluse it's 'far-reaching determination,' and when you're out in public life it's 'small grass.'"

Hsieh An appeared extremely embarrassed at this. But Huan Wen, glancing at him, laughed and said, "This statement by Aide-de-camp Hao isn't bad at that, and, you'll have to admit, it's extremely apt." (ch. 25, 446–47)

210. The two Ch'ihs (Ch'ih Yin and Ch'ih T'an) were devotees of the Tao, while the two Hos (Ho Ch'ung and Ho Chun) were devotees of the Buddha. Both made large contributions of money to gain merit. Hsieh Wan remarked, "The two Ch'ihs pay court to the Tao, while the two Hos fawn on the Buddha." (454)

211. The grand marshal, Wang Yen, once asked his son, Wang Hsüan, "Your uncle, Wang Ch'eng, is a famous gentleman. Why is it you don't admire or respect him?"

Hsüan replied, "Who ever heard of a famous gentleman who spends the whole day talking nonsense?" (ch. 26, 462)

212. Once when Ch'u P'ou was descending southward (toward the capital), Sun Ch'o saw him on board the boat, and in the course of their conversation they touched on Liu T'an's death (ca. 347). Sun wept profusely and took the occasion to chant the words (from the "Songs"):
"With this man's passing (*wang*),
The state has suffered sorely."
Ch'u, becoming very angry, replied, "In his whole life, when was Liu T'an ever compared with you? And yet now you're presenting this pose toward other people!"

Holding back his tears, Sun said to Ch'u, "You should remember me (too, when I'm gone)!" His contemporaries all laughed at him for being so talented, yet at the same time so vulgar by nature. (466)

213. Fan Wang as a person was fond of utilizing sagacious devices, but occasionally through excessive devising, he came to grief. (ch. 27, 483)

214. Yüan Yüeh was eloquent and capable in disquisitions on "short and long stratagems [*sic*]," and in addition possessed a refined power of reasoning. When he first became Hsieh Hsüan's aide he was treated with considerable deference. Later he lost one of his parents, and after the mourning period was ended and he had returned to the capital (Chien-k'ang), the only thing he carried about with him was the "Intrigues of the Warring States" (*Chan-kuo ts'e*) and nothing else. Speaking about it with others, he would say, "In my youth I used to study the 'Analects' (*Lun-yü*) and *Lao-tzu*, and I'd also look occasionally into *Chuang-tzu* and the 'Book of Changes' (*I*). Those all gave me a headache. What advantage do they offer? The most important work in the whole realm is precisely the 'Intrigues of the Warring States' (*Chan-kuo ts'e*)."

After coming to the capital he became advisor to the Prince of K'uai-chi, Ssu-ma Tao-tzu, by whom he was treated with the greatest intimacy. But after nearly subverting the very springs and pivot of government, he was suddenly executed (389). (ch. 32, 503)

215. Juan Yü was a follower of the Great Dharma (Mahayana Buddhism), in which his devotion and credulity went to extremes. When his eldest son, Juan Yung, was not yet twenty he was suddenly stricken by a severe illness. Since the boy was the one in whom all his love and honor were concentrated, Juan prayed on his behalf to the Three Treasures (the Buddha, the Dharma, and the Sangha), not slackening by day or by night, for he felt that if his utmost sincerity had any power

to move, he would surely receive help. But in the end the child did not recover, whereupon Juan bound himself to an eternal hatred of the Buddha, and all the devotion of his present and past lifetimes was totally wiped out. (ch. 33, 512)

216. As he was reclining on his bed Huan Wen once said, "If I keep on like this doing nothing (*dz'iek-dz'iek*), I'll be the laughingstock of Emperors Wen and Ching (Ssu-ma Chao and Ssu-ma Shih)." Then, after crouching and getting up from his seat, he continued, "Even if I can't let my fragrance be wafted down to later generations, does that mean I'm incapable of leaving behind a stench for ten thousand years?" (513)

***Officialdom Unmasked*, Li Boyuan, trans. and abr. T. L. Yang, Hong Kong UP, 2001**
217. The boy asked, 'What's my mistake?'
'Your father has only you as a son,' Teacher Wang patiently reasoned. 'Since he has ordered you to study, naturally he wants you to get ahead. In the future, you should be like your Brother Zhao and fight hard to attain the title of a Provincial Graduate.'
'What are the advantages of becoming a Provincial Graduate?' asked the boy.
'After one's reached this rank, he goes further and becomes a Metropolitan Graduate, and then he joins the Hanlin Academy. The advantages are limitless!' Wang Ren spoke enthusiastically.
'What in truth are those advantages?' the boy persisted.
'Once he becomes a member of the Hanlin Academy, he will be appointed an official,' Teacher Wang explained. 'Once he is an official, he will make money. He can even sit in court and have people beaten. When he goes out, his attendants precede him beating the gongs and shouting for others to make way. O-yo-yo! All these advantages! How are you going to get them if you do not study and pass the Provincial Examination?'
Though this boy was still very young, his heart began to stir when he heard that one could make a lot of money by becoming an official. Though he said nothing, he was beginning to be convinced.
After a short while, he asked again, 'Teacher, you are also a Provincial Graduate, why did you not become a Metropolitan Graduate and then an official?' (ch. 1)

218. Grandfather Zhao decided that his grandson's triumph called for a celebration which was a major undertaking. First, there were these attendants from the local Bureau of Announcements who had already ensconced themselves in groups of three to five at his residence. Each day, they demanded enormous quantities of meat and fish; and even the opium they consumed had to be provided by the Zhaos.
Then a guest-list was compiled, comprising relatives by marriage, fellow villagers, family friends and members of the same clan. He asked the bureau attendants to make copies of the list and delivered them to all those invited. Then he had to select an auspicious day for the making of sacrifices at the ancestral graves. Next, a chef and his team had to be engaged from the city, and it was ordered that whole pigs and whole lambs were to be served on the tables. Next, the services of musicians, masters of ceremony, and even technicians expert in letting off firecrackers were hired. Lastly, a lucky day for the banquet was decided on.
Boasting that since his grandson was now a Provincial Graduate, it was necessary for him to stay in close touch with all his fellow graduates of the same year, he ordered the carpenter to make six flagpoles, two to be erected in front of the family residence, two on the ancestral graves

and two at the ancestral hall. Then a horizontal wooden board was made, ideally for an Academician of the Hanlin Academy to write on it the three characters for 'Residence of Provincial Graduate'. However, after searching his mind, Grandfather Zhao still could not come up with a relative or friend of sufficient standing to perform the task. So he had to settle on Master Wang. (ibid.)

219. Teacher Wang wholeheartedly agreed, 'It is only for the sake of money that people are prepared to be an official even if it's a thousand *li* away from home!' (ch. 2)

220. The Police Chief is unlike the District Magistrate or Prefect who requires his escort and the beating of gongs whenever he goes out to announce that he is a great official. On the other hand, I could go out in plain clothes, and everyone knows who I am, I can enter an opium den as easily as I can enter a brothel or gambling house. All the people within the district are my people. So everyone must come and cultivate my patronage. If anyone should ignore me, well, nothing would be done if nothing goes wrong. But wait till something does happen, then I will deal with him strictly and show him no mercy! In the course of the year, there are two dates that cannot be ignored, my own birthday, and my wife's birthday. Next, come my father's birthday and my mother's birthday, my son's wedding and my daughter's wedding. So there are several of these occasions each year. On all these occasions, people will have to give me presents. The Police Chief relies on these celebrations to make a little money, which may amount to a good two thousand taels annually. So you must not fail to take these gifts into account. In fact, not only do I have no children, my parents have also passed away long before my term of office began. I only pretend that my family is at home in their native place and not staying with me. This way I could make the necessary excuse. The presents are offered because people give me face. There are other payments which have nothing to do with face-giving. Surely, it is not a crime for me to receive these payments. (Qian) (ibid.)

221. The truth of the matter was this. These impoverished officials in the Capital had no income unless they were given an assignment. Having waited patiently for three years before he was assigned an official mission, the Secretary hoped to recruit a few wealthy disciples so that his old debts could be repaid and credit for new debts could be obtained. (ibid.)

222. Nobody would believe it if one were not told! But the snobbery in official circles works as efficiently as Chang the Immortal's charms! Not so long ago, when a promotion was in the air, this house was clustered with carriages and horses; numberless people waited to see the great one but had to be disappointed. And now! There was not even a ghoul! (ch. 4)

223. Be that as it may, the substantive Governor had asked to come south and take up the post. And he would be arriving in a few days. This caused no great alarm for others, except the acting Lieutenant-Governor. Since he had arrived in the province only in an acting capacity, he had not dared to publicly sell any official positions which might fall vacant, for fear of attracting loose talk. Now that he heard the new Governor was soon to receive his seal of office, and he himself was obliged to return to his old post within days, he would not have long to enjoy his Lieutenant-Governorship.

Truly, greed causes one's intelligence to dim. So he bade the members of his staff and other trusted officials to canvass business for him here and there. The rule was that one thousand dollars was the minimum, and this amount would bring only a middle-ranking office. The best office required twenty thousand taels of silver, whoever had the money would succeed in the deal. It was a fair transaction, and there would be no favouritism. Some people had no ready cash, so this great official was prepared to accept a promissory note post-dated to the time the purchaser took up his position. (ibid.)

224. In this way, Tao had already spent three or four thousand on his new love. On making his calculations, he was comforted by the fact that he had only spent one-fourth of the twenty thousand he had brought with him. According to his plan, he would somehow insert these expenses into the invoices when he succeeded in buying the machinery. Thus reassured, he felt relieved and continued on squandering the money entrusted to him. (ch. 8)

225. People in the money-changer's are the most snobbish lot imaginable. Seeing that Tao had no money left, they cut him off and swore never to have any further dealings with him. (ibid.)

226. The gatekeeper said, 'Our lord has a chief wife and three concubines. Do you remember that there was an announcement issued two days ago? All payments for the purchase of offices must be made within two months. No more purchases may be made after two months. For this reason, our lord purchased an Intendancy for his chief wife's son. The first concubine's son comes second. Though he is only seven years of age, his mother also clamoured for an Intendancy for her son. The second concubine was envious when she heard this. Though she has no son, she is five months pregnant. She too insisted that our lord should purchase an office for the unborn son. His lordship said, "How do you know if the newborn baby is a boy or a girl? What if it is a girl?" The second concubine disagreed. She argued, "Of course we cannot be sure it will be a boy, nor can we be sure it will be a girl. Just make your purchase as a precaution. Even if the first-born is a girl, there will be a second-born!" His lordship was unable to contradict this argument, so he promised to make another purchase. But the office is one degree lower than an Intendancy, it is only a Prefectship. No sooner had he settled the dispute with the second concubine that the third concubine protested. She can't compare herself with the second concubine because she is not even pregnant. His lordship said, "You are not even conceived, what is your hurry?" She said, "Not now, but how do you know I shan't be next month?" So she too insisted that her husband should purchase the office of a Prefect.' (ch. 60)

"On Happiness," Qian Zhongshu, trans. Christopher G. Rea, in *Humans, Beasts, and Ghosts: Stories and Essays*, ed. Christopher G. Rea, Columbia UP, 2011
227. The presence of the character quick [*kuai*] in the words joy [*kuaihuo*] and happiness [*kuaile*], for instance, indicates the mutability of all delights with supreme clarity. So we say with a regretful sigh, "When joyful we find the night too short!" For when a person is happy life passes too quickly, but as soon as he encounters difficulty or boredom, time seems to move painfully slowly, as if dragging a lame foot. (43)

228. Happiness in life is like the sugar cube that entices the child to take his medicine, and even more so like the electric rabbit that lures dogs around the racetrack. For a few short minutes or days of happiness we endure a lifetime of suffering. We long for happiness to come, long for it to stay and long for it to come again—these three phrases sum up the history of mankind's endeavors. (44)

229. [C]ontradictions are the price of wisdom. This is life's big joke on philosophies of life. (46)

"On Laughter," Qian Zhongshu, trans. Christopher G. Rea, in *Humans, Beasts, and Ghosts: Stories and Essays*, ed. Christopher G. Rea, Columbia UP, 2011

230. Thus, humor is at most a sensibility. It most certainly cannot be branded as a doctrine, and it is even less well suited to being a profession. We must recall that the original Latin meaning of humor is "fluid." Put another way, humor, like woman in the eyes of Jia Baoyu, is made of water. To turn humor into a doctrine or a means of livelihood is to congeal a liquid into a solid, to transform a living thing into an artifact. When someone possessed of a genuine sense of humor starts selling laughter as his means of livelihood—Mark Twain, for instance—his works will no longer be worth reading. Since the end of the eighteenth century, Germans have loved to discourse on humor, but the more they've said, the less relevant the discussion has been to its ostensible topic. (49)

The Plum in the Golden Vase, or, Chin P'ing Mei, Hsiao-hsiao-sheng, trans. David Tod Roy, Princeton UP, 1993–2013

231. The hero grips his "Hook of Wu,"
Eager to cut off ten thousand heads.
How is it that a heart forged out of iron and stone,
Can yet be melted by a flower?

Just take a look at Hsiang Yü and Liu Pang:
Both cases are equally distressing.
They had only to meet with Yü-chi and Lady Ch'i,
For all their valor to come to naught. (v. 1, ch. 1)

232. Because the First Emperor of the Ch'in dynasty was so lacking in virtue that he:
    Garrisoned the Five Ranges to the south,
    Built the Great Wall to the north,
    Filled in the sea to the east,
    Constructed the O-pang Palace in the west,
    Swallowed up the Six States,
    Buried the scholars alive, and
    Burned the books,
Hsiang Yü rose up in rebellion against him and was joined by the King of Han, whose name was Liu Chi, or Liu Pang. (ibid.)

233. Now why do you suppose your narrator is so preoccupied with explicating the two words passion and beauty? It is because "Gentlemen who presume on their talents are lacking in virtue, and women who flaunt their beauty are dissolute." (ibid.)

234. The story goes that during the years of the Cheng-ho reign period of Emperor Hui-tsung of the Sung dynasty, the emperor bestowed his trust and favor upon the four wicked ministers, Kao Ch'iu, Yang Chien, T'ung Kuan, and Ts'ai Ching, with the result that the empire was thrown into great disorder. The people were unable to pursue their vocations and the populace was in dire

straits. On all sides bandits arose in swarms and baleful stars descended to earth to be incarnated in human form. The glittering facade presented by the empire of the Great Sung dynasty was disrupted, and in four different places great bandit chieftains arose. (ibid.)

235. Gentle reader take note:
> In this world the heart of man alone
>   remains vile.
> It despises the weak,
> While fearing the wicked.
> If it's too hard it's brittle;
> If it's too soft it's no use. (ibid.)

236. Chin-lien's dream of clouds and rain
>   did not materialize;
> Who would believe that this evoked
>   hostility in her heart?
> Thus did she contrive to get Wu Sung
>   out of the way;
> And sow enmity between brothers
>   of the same flesh and blood. (ibid.)

237. "If you want me to protect you," said Dame Wang, "I've got a plan that should do the trick. Do you want to be 'long-term man and wife' or 'short-term man and wife'?"

"Godmother," said Hsi-men Ch'ing, "what do you mean by 'long-term man and wife' and 'short-term man and wife'?"

"If you want to be 'short-term man and wife,'" said Dame Wang, "you should separate from each other this very day, wait until Wu the Elder has recovered, and offer him an apology. Then, when Wu the Second comes back, he won't say anything about it, and you can wait until he's sent away on another mission to get together again. That's what I mean by 'short term man and wife.' But if you want to be 'long-term man and wife,' to spend every day together without having to:
> Anticipate surprise and suffer fear,
I've got a splendid plan for you. The only thing is it's not an easy subject to broach."

"Godmother," said Hsi-men Ch'ing, "please help us out. The only thing we want is to be 'long-term man and wife.'" . . .

"Right now," said Dame Wang, "this 'knockabout' is in pretty bad shape. This presents you with the opportunity to take action against him while he's incapacitated. You, sir, should go home and pick up some arsenic from your pharmaceutical shop and then get the young lady to buy a dose of heart medicine, mix the arsenic in with it, and polish off this runt once and for all. If you cremate the body afterward you'll have gotten him completely out of the way, without leaving a trace behind. Then, even if Wu the Second comes back, what will he be able to do about it?" (ch. 5)

238. Gentle reader take note: The matchmakers of this world are not really interested in anything but making money for themselves. What do they care whether their clients end up dead or alive? They will describe a marriage prospect who holds no office as an officeholder, and a position as

concibine as though it were a position as legitimate wife. They are such inveterate liars they would attempt to deceive Heaven itself, and there is no truth whatever to be found in their asseverations. (ch. 7)

239. "Spread a little extra money around, high and low," the woman advised Hsi-men Ch'ing. "See to it that they finish him off, so there'll be no danger of his ever getting free again."

Hsi-men Ch'ing sent his trusted servant, Lai-wang, to convey a set of gold and silver wine vessels and fifty taels of "snowflake" silver to the district magistrate. He also distributed a good deal of additional money, high and low, to the other functionaries, including the docket officer. The only purpose behind this largess was to see to it that Wu the Second was not treated leniently. The district magistrate accepted Hsi-men Ch'ing's bribe. (ch. 10)

240. If you're clever, you'll be considered labored,
        if you're awkward, idle;
If you're good, you'll be disdained as weak,
        if you're bad, callous.
If you're rich, you'll meet with envy,
        if you're poor, disgrace;
If you're diligent, you'll be thought grasping,
        if you're economical, stingy.
If you deal with things consistently,
        you'll be scorned as simple;
If you adapt yourself to circumstances,
        you'll be suspected of deceit.
If you think about it, it is hardly possible
        to satisfy anyone;
The role of human being is an arduous one,
        to be a man is hard. (v. 2, ch. 22)

241. Gentle reader take note: Most of the adulterous women of this world, no matter how smart their husbands are, even if they are tough enough to chew nails, can get around them with a few phrases that:
        Misstate wrong as right,
so effectively that nine out of ten of them are deceived. Truly:
        Like the bricks in the privy:
        They're both hard and smelly. (ch. 25)

242. Success and failure, flourishing and decay,
        are all inconsequential;
To deploy every device at your disposal
        is likewise of no avail.
Human desires are never satisfied, like
        a snake swallowing an elephant;
The affairs of this world, in the end, are like
        a mantis seizing a cicada.
There is no medicine that is able to cure

the aging of high officials;
No amount of money will purchase the virtue
  of one's sons and grandsons.
To rest content with one's ordinary lot
  and take things as they come;
Is the way to enjoy a carefree life of
  free and easy wandering. (ch. 30)

243. Gentle reader take note: At that time, during the reign of emperor Hui-tsung:
  The empire was badly governed;
  Wicked ministers held positions of power,
  Slanderers and sycophants filled the court.
The four wicked ministers, Kao Ch'iu, Yang Chien, T'ung Kuan, and Ts'ai Ching, presided at court:
  Selling offices and bartering justice,
  Flagrantly trafficking in bribes;
  Promoting officials with scales in hand,
  Pointing to the post and demanding the price.
Those who resorted to:
  Truckling and insinuation,
  Rapidly rose to high position.
Those who were:
  Worthy, able, honest, and straightforward,
  Went for years without appointment.
As a result,
  Public mores deteriorated.
  Venal officials and corrupt functionaries,
  Overspread the entire empire.
  The burdens of corvée and taxation were heavy,
  The people were impoverished and bandits arose.
  The empire was ripe for revolt.
  Solely because the wicked and sycophantic
   occupied positions of power,
  It was only appropriate that the Central Plain
   should become soaked in blood. (ibid.)

244. One may find things less than satisfactory
  eight or nine times out of ten;
But it is seldom wise to tell anyone about
  even two or three of them. (ibid.)

245. On a white horse with bloodied trappings
  he [Hsi-men Ch'ing] is newly caparisoned;
Even those with no claim to relationship
  insist on being related.
When fortune comes, even the crudest iron

looks shiny;
When luck recedes, even the truest gold
   lack luster. (ch. 31)

246. Frivolous and flighty by nature,
   His words overstate the facts.
   Possessed of a clever tongue,
   He is a glib conversationalist.
   Those to whom he promises money, end up
   Catching at shadows and clutching the wind;
   But bilking others of their due, he finds
   As easy as groping for something in a bag.
For these reasons, the people in his neighborhood, observing how meretricious he was, casually referred to him as Posturer Han. (ch. 33)

247. He whose hatred is petty is no gentleman;
He who lacks ruthlessness is not a hero. (ch. 35)

248. If you're going to be a human being,
   don't be a woman;
Or your every joy and sorrow will be
   dependent on another.
It's the old story of the, "Fond female
   and the fickle fellow";
If only she hadn't taken him so seriously
   to begin with. (ibid.)

249. It is said that young scholars have always been
   frivolous in their affections;
And here he is flirting with a dainty maiden
   from a good family. *(v. 3, ch. 41)*

250. Li Kuei-chieh did not arrive until the following day, and when she saw that Wu Yin-erh was already there, she surreptitiously asked Yüeh-niang, "How long has she been here?"
      Yüeh-niang told her, thus and so, "Yesterday she brought gifts and paid obeisance to the Sixth Lady in order to be acknowledged as her adopted daughter."
      When Li Kuei-chieh heard this, she hadn't a word to say, but she was huffy with Wu Yin-erh all day long, the two of them refusing to speak to each other. (ch. 42)

251. The problem is that the others, on seeing that you have given birth to a son, can't help being somewhat put out. (Wu Yin-erh) (ch. 44)

252. Wang Liu-erh peddles influence in pursuit of profit; Hsi-men Ch'ing accepts a bribe and subverts the law (chapter title) (ch. 47)

253. Now this Miao Ch'ing held a deep grudge against his master, Miao T'ien-hsiu, for the beating he had previously received at his hands. He had wanted to get revenge for some time but had not had an opportunity to do so.

> From his mouth no word was uttered, but
> In his heart he thought to himself,

"Why don't I:

> Thus and thus, and
> So and so,

collaborate with these two boatmen in seizing my master, killing him, shoving his body into the water, and then dividing his property between us? If I return home and manage to plot the death of his invalid wife, his whole estate, together with his concubine, née Tiao, will all be mine." (ch. 47)

254. When Chai Ch'ien had read Hsi-men Ch'ing's letter, he said, "Censor Tseng's bill of impeachment has not yet been delivered, so you had better stick around for a few days. At present, the situation here is that His Honor has just submitted a memorial laying out proposals with regard to seven matters, but the imperial rescript in response to it has not yet come down. You might as well wait until this document comes down. After that, when Censor Tseng's memorial arrives, I'll be able to speak to him about it, and get him to issue a verbal notation in the Grand Secretariat, ordering that it be:

> Directed to the attention of the appropriate board.

On my part, I'll then send someone with my card, instructing the minister of war, Yü Shen, to suppress the memorial so that it is not resubmitted. Your master can relax. I guarantee that nothing will ever come of it." (ch. 48)

255. At this juncture, Tseng Hsiao-hsü was turned over to the Ministry of Personnel for investigation, and subsequently demoted to the position of prefect of Ch'ing-chou in Shensi. The regional investigating censor of Shensi at the time was Sung Sheng-ch'ung, who was the elder brother of Ts'ai Yu's wife. Ts'ai Ching secretly suborned him into traducing Tseng Hsiao-hsü for an alleged private transgression, as a result of which his servants were arrested and:

> Tortured into giving evidence to substantiate the case.

Ts'ai Ching consequently succeeded in having him removed from office and:

> Banished to the southern extremity of the country,

in order to accomplish his revenge. (ch. 49)

256. There is a poem, designed to explicate the difficulties that human feelings make for people, which goes as follows:

> Justice and human feelings are
>   frequently in conflict;
> Human feelings and justice are
>   difficult to reconcile.
> If one insists upon doing justice,
>   human feelings will suffer;
> If one gives way to human feelings,
>   justice will lose out. (ibid.)

257. Impressed by her proclivity for:

> Raising her brows and batting her eyes,
>
> Assuming attitudes and putting on airs;

and observing that she was given to:

> Hairsplitting and logic-chopping;

in speaking to her, the words "Reverend Hsüeh" were seldom out of their mouths; while she, in turn, addressed Yüeh-niang with the words "Lay Bodhisattva," or "My Lady." (ch. 50)

258. Hsi-men Ch'ing then said to the woman, "When your husband gets home, I'll send him to Yang-chou, along with Lai-pao and Ts'ui Pen, in order to take delivery of a consignment of salt. Then, after they have taken delivery of the salt, and sold it, I'll send him to Hu-chou to arrange a shipment of woven silk goods. How would that be?"

"My good daddy!" exclaimed the woman, "Send him wherever you want, just so he's out of the way. What's the point of keeping the cuckold idle at home?" (ibid.)

259. As the saying goes:

> You may peddle a load of truths for ten days
>
> > without making a sale;
>
> While, in a single day, a load of falsehoods
>
> > will actually sell out. (ibid.)

260. The story goes that when P'an Chin-lien realized that Hsi-men Ch'ing had taken the bag of sexual implements and gone to spend the night in Li P'ing-erh's quarters, she was so upset that she was unable to sleep all night long and secretly stored up resentment in her heart.

The next day, upon learning that Hsi-men Ch'ing had gone to the yamen, and that Li P'ing-erh was still combing her hair in her quarters, she lost no time in going back to the rear compound, where she said to Yüeh-niang, "Li P'ing-erh has been criticizing you severely behind your back. She said, 'Elder Sister puts on the airs of a grande dame, ordering people around as though she were holding court. It was someone else's birthday, but you insisted on taking charge. It was your husband who got drunk and came into my quarters when I was not there, but you shamed me before the others for no good reason, causing me to lose face. I was so upset by this that I went back up front and insisted that Father return to the rear compound, but after a while, somehow or other, he didn't remain there, but chose to come back to my quarters.' The two of them engaged in intimate conversation all night long and managed to expose everything but their hearts and entrails to me in the process."

When Yüeh-niang heard this, how could she help but be upset. (ch. 51)

261. Only after Hsiao-yü had brought in the tea did Yüeh-niang get up and sit disconsolately in her room, saying to herself, "Simply because I don't have a son of my own, I have to put up with all this annoyance at other people's hands. I have:

> Besought Heaven and worshipped Earth,

in the hope of obtaining one, so that I can shame those lousy whores to their fucking faces." (ch. 53)

262. Though you may have money enough to worship
  the Northern Dipper,

Who is able to buy a guarantee that nothing
   untoward will happen? (ch. 58)

263. This P'an Chin-lien, having been aware for some time that ever since Li P'ing-erh had borne Kuan-ko, Hsi-men Ch'ing had been:
   Obedient to her every whim,
that:
   Whatever she asked for, she received tenfold,
and that every day she was:
   Contending in beauty and competing for favor,
had developed feelings of jealousy and anger in her heart over this favoritism. On this day, therefore, she had deliberately set this secret plot in motion, training her cat for the purpose, out of a desire to frighten her rival's child to death, and thereby diminish Li P'ing-erh's favor, and cause Hsi-men Ch'ing to resume his intimacy with her. (ch. 59)

264. "Though I did not venture to say so just now," said Old Man Ho, "this fellow is well-known outside the East Gate as Chao the Quack. All he knows how to do is:
   Sport placards and rattle his bell,
on the streets, attempting to con the passersby. What does he know about pulse diagnosis or the etiology of disorders?" (v. 4, ch. 61)

265. On this occasion, when Hsi-men Ch'ing rejoined his guests in the summer-house, he told the assembled officials all about how the regional investigating censor Sung Ch'iao-nien was planning to lead the officials of the Two Provincial Offices and eight prefectures in welcoming Defender-in-chief Huang Ching-ch'en next month and had asked him to provide a reception in his honor.
   On hearing this, the assembled officials, with one voice, said, "This visit will entail insuperable tribulation for the prefectures and districts involved. When such imperial emissaries come, all of the expenses for the attending personnel, provisions, public banquets, utensils, and corvée laborers are borne by the prefectures and districts, which, in turn, must extract them from the people. As a way of bringing about the utter depletion of both public and private resources:
   Nothing could surpass this.
We all hope, Ssu-ch'üan, that you will put in a good word with your superiors on our behalf in order to alleviate our plight. That would constitute a signal demonstration of our mutual esteem." (ch. 65)

266. "Mother," said Chin-lien, "I also have noticed how that woman has altered her demeanor the last few days. I fear that that lousy shameless good-for-nothing of ours, who has been spending all day in her quarters, is making out with that woman. It would hardly surprise me. I've heard that, the other day, he gave her two pairs of ornamental hairpins, and that the woman has had the effrontery to wear them on her head, showing them off, first to this one, and then to that one."
   "Bean sprouts don't lend themselves to being bundled,"
said Yüeh-niang.
   Thus it was that, behind their backs, everyone:
   Conveyed the clear impression that they were not happy. (ibid.)

267. One day, you may swear to live your lives together,
But, one night, your oath will vanish like a cloud.
Her flying phoenix golden hairpin will tumble out,
The soaring phoenix precious mirror will fracture.
Your delight in her salvation will prove ephemeral,
While your lasting mortification will not diminish.
Only by frequent resort to the contents of the cup,
Can you gain temporary relief from your affliction. (ch. 66)

268. Gentle reader take note: black-clad Buddhist nuns of this ilk ought never to be patronized under any circumstances.

> Their faces may be like the faces of nuns,
> But their hearts are the hearts of whores.

It is simply the case that:

> Their six senses are unpurified,
> Their basic natures are unclear,
> Their vows are entirely ignored,
> Their sense of shame is effaced.
> Though falsely boasting of their compassion,
> They are driven entirely by profit and lust.
> Ignoring karma and the wheel of transmigration,
> They think solely of the pleasure of the moment.
> Having inveigled the frustrated young maidens
>   of humbler households,
> They set their sights on the susceptible wives
>   of prominent families.
> At their front doors they welcome
>   benefactors and donors,
> At the back doors they dispose of
>   their unwanted fetuses.
> When not promoting illicit liaisons,
> They are devising adulterous trysts. (ch. 68)

269. Manifestly, he was:

> A wealthy but untrustworthy, crafty
>   and treacherous person;
> An abuser of the innocent and good,
>   addicted to wine and sex. (ch. 69)

270. Yüeh-niang responded, "Why don't you:

> Piddle a bladderful of piss, and
> Take a look at your own reflection?

You're like:

> A raven scoffing at the blackness of a pig.

Truly:

> The lampstand casts no light upon itself.

You may well think you have the capacity to amount to something yourself, but:

> You too have drunk water from that well.
> There's nothing you won't do.

What's so pure about your own conduct that you should have the right to criticize the conduct of others?"

With these few words she managed to reduce Hsi-men Ch'ing to silence. (ibid.)

271. In humorous conversation they initiate hostilities;
With idle boasts they disturb the national safety.
When they issue spurious decrees,
The eight chief officials in the realm
    bow in acquiescence;
When they employ clever arguments,
The Emperor in his nine-gated palace
    nods his head in consent.
By initiating the Flower and Rock Convoys,
He has inflicted calamity upon the Chiang-nan
    and the Huai-pei regions;
By seizing boxwood to offer to the throne,
He has exhausted both the national treasury
    and the people's resources.
Among those who serve at court there are none
    whose hearts have not been chilled;
Among the ranks of men of integrity there are
    none who are not holding their breath. (ch. 70)

272. As I was saying, in the future, you ought to amend the reckless way you go about your business. As the sayings go:

> On first meeting one should express no more than
>   three-tenths of one's thoughts;
> Never under any circumstances should one disclose
>   the whole content of one's heart.
> Even one's wife may harbor duplicitous intent,
> Not to mention people in the world at large. (Yüeh-niang) (ch. 72)

273. If you wish to get along, say what people want to hear;
If you try to be honest, you'll only arouse antagonism.
In the affairs of this world, it is best to be lukewarm;
People's true sentiments become apparent only with time. (ibid.)

274. "Fifth Lady," said Kuei-chieh, "you don't understand the nature of people in our profession, who are given to taking out their anger on one another."

Yüeh-niang picked up where she left off, saying, "What is the difference between you denizens of the quarter and the rest of us? We are all alike in that when we get angry with each other, the one with the most favor will trample the other underfoot." (ch. 74)

275. Before anyone could stop her [Ch'un-mei], like a whirlwind, she swept into the master suite, pointed her finger at Second Sister Shen, and began a tirade against her, saying, "How dare you say of me to a page boy that 'another young lady has emerged out of nowhere,' or express amazement that I should have the nerve to order you around? Are you the wife of some regional commander, that I would not dare send for? Whose cunt do you suppose I was squeezed out of, only to be sized up by the likes of you, who pronounce that I've emerged out of nowhere? As for you, you're nothing but a lousy dog-fucked blind whore, who frequents:
> The doors of a thousand households,
> The gates of ten thousand families.
How long have you been coming to this household, that you have the audacity to evaluate its members? And what kind of presentable song suites are you able to perform?" (ch. 75)

276. "As the saying goes," said Sister-in-law Wu:
> "No good blows are struck when people fight;
> No good words are spoken when people quarrel." (ch. 75)

277. Since I was taken into your household merely to be your concubine, my status is unpropitious. It has always been true that
> Good people are subject to being gulled;
> Good horses are subject to being ridden.
That's just the way it is. (Chin-lien) (ch. 76)

278. After dismissing the accusation against Ho the Tenth and setting him free, he [Hsi-men Ch'ing] proceeded to arrest a monk from the Hung-hua Temple to take his place, on the trumped up charge that he had sheltered the thieves in his temple overnight. Can there actually be such cases of injustice in this world? Truly:
> Mr. Chang drinks wine, but Mr. Li
>   gets drunk;
> The mulberry branch is cut with a knife,
>   but the willow bark is scarred.
There is a poem that testifies to this:
> The destiny of the Sung dynasty was
>   coming to an end;
> The holders of judicial appointments
>   were so dishonest. (ibid.)

279. Today, after obtaining their depositions, I [His-men Ch'ing] have had them remanded to Tung-p'ing prefecture. Once they get there, since they are guilty of the crime of fornication between a son-in-law and mother-in-law, thus falling within the fifth degree of mourning relationships, the penalty for both parties is strangulation." (ibid.)

280. In painting a tiger, you can paint the skin,
>   but you can't paint the bones;
> In knowing people, you can know their faces,
>   but you can't know their hearts. (Hsi-men Ch'ing) (ibid.)

281. Gentle reader take note:
> Only at intervals is the bright moon full;
> The variegated clouds are easily dispersed.
> When joy reaches its zenith, it gives birth to sorrow;
> The nadir will be followed by the zenith.
> This is a self-evident principle.

Hsi-men Ch'ing was only bent on:
> Competing for prestige and usurping profit;
> Indulging his desires and slaking his lust.

He was utterly oblivious to the fact that, since:
> The Way of Heaven is inimical to excess;
> The recorders of Hell were on his heels,
> And the hour of his death was impending. (ch. 78)

282. Meng Yü-lou told Li Chiao-erh to tend to Yüeh-niang while she went out and dispatched a page boy to go as quickly as possible to summon Midwife Ts'ai. Li Chiao-erh also sent Yü-hsiao to the front compound to summon Ju-i. By the time Meng Yü-lou returned to Yüeh-niang's room, Li Chiao-erh had disappeared. It so happens that Li Chiao-erh, taking advantage of Yüeh-niang's unconscious state, had noticed that the trunk was open and had surreptitiously taken out five silver ingots worth fifty taels apiece and carried them off to her quarters. (ch. 79)

283. Only when gold is subjected to smelting
    is its quality assessed;
Only when humans are tempted by riches
    are their hearts exposed. (ibid.)

284. After our death, who knows what will be
    our final destination?
Every last thing that we possess, we are
    unable to take with us;
Without so much as a stitch of clothing
    we must face King Yama. (ch. 80)

285. Wine does not befuddle people, they
    befuddle themselves.
Beauty does not delude people, they
    delude themselves. (v. 5, ch. 81)

286. Gentle reader take note: All families with good boys and good girls should be sure never to deliver them to Buddhist monasteries or Taoist temples to leave the family and become monks or priests, Buddhist nuns or Taoist priestesses. Once exposed to those:
> Male thieves and female whores,
nine out of ten of them are likely to be victimized. There is a poem that testifies to this.

> For what purpose are Taoist sanctuaries and
>   Buddhist temples established?

The Taoists worship their Heavenly Worthies,
    the Buddhists worship Buddha.
They are beautifully landscaped in order to
    give a false sense of purity;
Providing for visitors and welcoming guests
    they engage in perverse doings.
Accoutering their disciples with attractive
    clothes and handsome outfits;
They make use of wanton wine and leisured tea
    in ravishing female beauties.
How sad that the tenderly nurtured offspring
    of respectable families;
Should be entrusted to such monastics only to
    serve as their concubines. (ch. 82)

287. It so happens that this Ch'ing-feng Mountain had a stronghold called the Ch'ing-feng Stronghold located on it that housed three outlaw chieftains, one of whom was called the Brocade Tiger, Yen Shun; one of whom was called the Short-legged Tiger, Wang Ying; and one of whom was called the Palefaced Gentleman, Cheng T'ien-shou. They had a troop of five hundred followers serving under them who devoted themselves solely to:
        Housebreaking and highway robbery,
        Setting fires and killing people,
so that no one dared to interfere with them. (ch. 84)

288. In this world the heart of man alone
    remains vile;
In all things demanding that Heaven
    show him favor. (ibid.)

289. The trouble of bringing up daughters is
    bound to be disillusioning;
To admit their husbands into the family
    is even more inappropriate.
They may address their in-laws as parents,
    but without genuine feeling;
They may choose to play the part of sons,
    but their acting is specious.
On entering your home they will complain
    of receiving inadequate love;
On leaving your household they are more
    likely than not to hate you.
If they feel that they are not receiving
    the treatment they deserve;
They can be counted upon to abuse their
    spouses at least once a day. (ch. 85)

290. Only regard the customs of the age
   as illusory performances;
While respecting the intentions of others
   by keeping them at a distance.
If one were to address perceptive women with
   a word to the wise;
It would be, "Don't ever confide your troubles
   to your sweetheart." (ch. 86)

291. I have heard that this police chief Wu Tien-en used to work as a manager in their household. It was only because he was sent by his employer to deliver some gifts to Grand Preceptor Ts'ai Ching in the Eastern Capital that he was able to obtain this office. How can he do such an about-face and bring a false accusation against his former benefactors? (the commandant) (ch. 95)

The Poetry of T'ao Ch'ien, trans. James Robert Hightower, Clarendon, 1970
292. Alas, the sycophants and slanders—
The world abhors anything superior.
The man of vision they call deluded,
The one whose conduct is upright they say is perverse.
He who is absolutely righteous and above suspicion
In the end is put to shame with slanderous charges.
You may clasp your jewel and cling to your orchids,
In vain your fragrance and purity—who believes in them? ("Lament for Gentlemen Born Out of Their Time," 261)

"A Prejudice," Qian Zhongshu, trans. Christopher G. Rea, in *Humans, Beasts, and Ghosts: Stories and Essays*, ed. Christopher G. Rea, Columbia UP, 2011
293. Perhaps we could say that "man is the animal that makes noise whether day or night, winter or summer." (64)

Records of the Grand Historian: Han Dynasty I, rev. ed., Sima Qian, trans. Burton Watson, Columbia UP, 1993
294. During the hundred years after the founding of the Han these various branches of the imperial family became increasingly estranged from the central court. Some among the feudal lords grew arrogant and extravagant, and were misled by the schemes of vicious minsters [*sic*] into evil and insubordination. The most powerful among them rebelled, while the lesser ones committed violations of the law, endangering their lives and bringing ruin upon themselves and their states. (intros. to *Shi ji*, 17, 18 and 19, 424–25)

Records of the Grand Historian: Han Dynasty II, rev. ed., Sima Qian, trans. Burton Watson, Columbia UP, 1993
295. The Grand Historian remarks: . . . But when it comes to men like Feng Dang, the governor of Shu, who violently oppressed the people; Li Zhen of Guanghan who tore people limb from limb for his own pleasure; Mi Pu of Dong Province who sawed people's heads off; Luo Bi of Tianshui who bludgeoned people into making confessions; Chu Guang of Hedong who executed people

indiscriminately; Wu Ji of the capital and Yin Zhou of Fengyi who ruled like vipers or hawks; or Yan Feng of Shuiheng who beat people to death unless they bribed him for their release—why bother to describe all of them? Why bother to describe all of them? ("*Shi ji* 122: The Biographies of the Harsh Officials," 407)

296. Lao Zi has said that under the ideal form of government, "though states exist side by side, so close that they can hear the crowing of each other's cocks and the barking of each other's dogs, the people of each state will savour their own food, admire their own clothing, be content with their own customs, and delight in their own occupations, and will grow old and die without ever wandering abroad." Yet if one were to try to apply this type of government, striving to drag the present age back to the conditions of primitive times and to stop up the eyes and ears of the people, it is doubtful that one would have much chance of success!

   The Grand Historian remarks: I know nothing about the times of Shen Nong and before but, judging by what is recorded in the *Odes* and *Documents,* from the age of Emperor Shun and the Xia dynasty down to the present, ears and eyes have always longed for the ultimate in beautiful sounds and forms, mouths have desired to taste the best in grass-fed and grain-fed animals, bodies have delighted in ease and comfort, and hearts have swelled with pride at the glories of power and ability. So long have these habits been allowed to permeate the lives of the people that, though one were to go from door to door preaching the subtle arguments of the Taoists, he could never succeed in changing them. ("*Shi ji* 129: The Biographies of the Money-makers," 433–34)

***Records of the Three States: The Book of Wei*, Chen Shou, trans. Robert Joe Cutter and William Gordon Crowell, in *Empresses and Consorts: Selections from Chen Shou's* Records of the Three States *with Pei Songzhi's Commentary*, U. of Hawai'i Press, 1999**
297. The [*Apocryphon to the*] *Spring and Autumn Annals: Explaining* [*the Themes and Words*] says that the Son of Heaven has twelve women and the nobles have nine. If one looks into it, this is a sound rule in terms of both emotion and reason. But later ages were extravagant and undisciplined and indulged their wasteful desires to the point that it left men and women pining and single and affected and shook the spirit of harmony. They only exalted sex and did not take pure goodness as basic. Therefore, customs and moral teaching deteriorated, and the major relationships were destroyed. (5.155, 89)

298. Lady Pan was by nature wickedly jealous of other charmers. From beginning to end, she slandered a great many, including Lady Yuan and others. When Sun Quan was not well, Lady Pan sent someone to enquire of Prefect of the Palace Writers Sun Hong the precedent of Empress Lü's assumption of power. She was exhausted from attending to Quan's illness and as a result became emaciated. A number of courtiers, taking advantage of her being in a deep sleep, strangled her and attributed her death to a sudden illness. Later, the matter leaked out and six or seven persons were sentenced to death. (50.1199, 128–29)

***The Republic of Wine: A Novel*, Mo Yan, trans. Howard Goldblatt, Arcade, 2012**
299. The most glorious events invariably incorporate elements of the most despicable nature. (ch. 3)

300. That is how children are: they will gang up on a poor frog, or a snake crossing the road, or a wounded cat. And after beating it half to death, they'll crowd around to enjoy the spectacle. (ibid.)

301. In this world, one should never be too conscientious about anything; it's a sure path to bad luck. (ch. 4)

302. If you must know, no biographer worth his salt would waste time interviewing individuals, since ninety percent of what's gleaned through interviews is lies and fabrications. What you need to do is separate the real from the false, arrive at the truth by seeing what lies behind all those lies and fabrications. (ch. 5)

303. Everyone has his own problems, and talking about them doesn't help—the hungry man's belly is just as empty, the thirsty man's mouth stays just as dry. (ch. 7)

304. In this day and age, everything is adulterated. Even the swallow has learned the trick. In my view, ten thousand years down the road, if humans are still around, swallows will be using dog shit to build their nests. (ibid.)

305. Besides, drinking liquor, as with the consumption of all food and drink, is a habit that becomes a mania: always preferring something new over something old, always ready to take a risk, always seeking a more intense high. Much gourmandism results from anti-traditionalism and a disdain for the law. When one tires of eating fresh, white tofu, one turns to moldy, gummy, stinky tofu or pickled tofu; when one tires of eating fresh, tasty pork, one dines on rotten, maggot-ridden meat. Following that logic, when one tires of imbibing ambrosial spirits and jadelike brews, one seeks out strangely bitter or spicy or sour or dank flavors to excite the taste buds and the membranes of the mouth. So long as we lead the way, there isn't a liquor made we can't sell to the public. (ch. 9)

Rickshaw Boy: A Novel, Lao She, trans. Howard Goldblatt, Harper Perennial, 2010
306. Xiangzi had worked for both civilian and military employers; none of the military employers had been the equal of Fourth Master Liu, while among the civilian employers, which included university lecturers and officials with good jobs in the official yamen, all well-educated individuals, none was a man of reason. And for those who came close, their wives and daughters made life difficult for him. (ch. 7)

307. But when it became clear that neither party would give ground, they made themselves scarce at the first opportunity. As the saying goes, "An upright official steers clear of domestic disputes." (ch. 15)

308. The compound was home to seven or eight families, most of whom packed a dozen or more people into a single room. . . . The days were hardest on the elderly and the women. . . . Clad in rags and with a bowl or less of gruel in their stomachs, the heavily pregnant women did their work only after everyone else was fed, with wind whistling in through holes in one wall and carrying all the warmth out of the tiny rooms through cracks in another. Riddled with disease, these women had lost most of their hair before they reached the age of thirty, but they worked on, from sickness to death, when they were buried in coffins paid for by charitable people in the community. Girls

of sixteen or seventeen, having no trousers to wear, simply wrapped a tattered cloth around themselves and did not venture outside—for them the rooms were virtual prisons where they helped their mothers with their chores. If they needed to visit the latrine, they first made sure that the compound was deserted before slipping outside unnoticed. They did not see the sun or blue sky all winter long. The ugly ones would take over for their mothers in time, while the decent-looking girls knew that sooner or later they would be sold by their parents to enjoy a good life, as they say. (ch. 16)

309. No wonder Er Qiangzi turned to drink and his down-and-out friends committed all kinds of outrages. Pulling a rickshaw was a dead-end trade. No matter how hard you worked or tried to better yourself, you cannot marry, get sick, or make a false move. (ch. 19)

310. After an hour, she returned out of breath. Supporting herself on the table, she was racked by coughs before she could speak. A visit by the doctor would cost ten yuan for a quick examination, she reported. The childbirth would cost twenty more. And a difficult delivery would require taking the patient to the hospital, which would mean much more money.
    "What should we do, Elder Brother?"
    There was nothing they *could* do but wait for death to claim whom it would.
    Ignorance and cruelty had brought them to this point. Where there is ignorance and where there is cruelty, there will be other reasons.
    At midnight, Huniu delivered a dead infant and then stopped breathing. (ibid.)

311. This job was located in the vicinity of the Yonghe Lamasery. His employer, a fellow in his fifties named Xia, was an educated, cultured man with a wife and twelve children. He had recently taken a concubine, without his wife's knowledge, and had installed her in this quiet part of the city. Only four occupants lived in the new household: Mr. Xia, his concubine, a maidservant, and the rickshaw man—Xiangzi. (ch. 20)

312. "You thought you could make it on your own, didn't you?" the old man said, reacting to Xiangzi's sad tale. "That's what everybody thinks, and what no one manages to do. I was young and strong once, and ready to take on the world. But look at me now. Would you call me strong? Even for a man of steel there's no way out of the net we're all caught in. Good intentions? A waste of time. Good is rewarded with good, and evil with evil, they say, but don't you believe it! When I was young, I was known as a warmhearted, helpful person who always looked out for others. Did that do me any good? None. I even saved someone from drowning once and one from hanging. My reward? Nothing. I tell you, I could freeze to death one of these days. I now know that for poor, hardworking people there's nothing more difficult than making it on their own." (Little Ma's grandfather) (ch. 23)

313. The way I see it, one of two things happened. Either Er Qiangzi sold her to be someone's concubine or she's been sent to the White Manor. The second possibility is more likely. Why do I say that? If, as you say, she's been married before, finding a man who'll want her now won't be easy. Men expect their concubines to be virgins. So I'm guessing she wound up in the White Manor. I'm nearly sixty, and I've seen a lot in my time. If a healthy young rickshaw man doesn't show up on the street for a couple of days, you'll find that he's either landed a monthly job or he's made his way to the White Manor. And if the wife or daughter of one of the rickshaw men disappears

all of a sudden, chances are that's where you'll find them. We sell our sweat; our women sell their bodies. That's something I know. (Little Ma's grandfather) (ibid.)

314. Those who took part in the fairs or just went to watch experienced the same enthusiasm, piety, and excitement. During troubled times, superstition spawns bustling activity, and the ignorant find consolation only in self-deception. The array of colors and sounds, the pristine clouds, and the dusty streets imbued the populace with energy and drive. Some climbed the mountain, some visited temples, and others took in flower shows . . . those too poor to do any of that could still stand by the road and watch the excitement or recite a Buddhist chant or two. (ch. 24)

315. . History is replete with the likes of the rebel leaders Huang Chao and Zhang Xianzhong and the bloodthirsty Taipings, who not only slaughtered victims but also took pleasure in seeing people slaughtered. A firing squad seemed too commonplace, nowhere near as much fun to watch as the death of a thousand cuts, beheadings, or skinning or burying alive; the mere sound of these punishments produced the same shuddering enjoyment as eating ice cream. But this time, before they shot him they were going to parade him through the streets; whoever thought that up was to be congratulated, since this was a rare opportunity to feast their eyes on a half-dead, trussed-up man in the back of a truck. That was the next best thing to being the executioner himself. Such people are not burdened by a sense of right and wrong, an understanding of good and evil, or a grasp of what is true and what is false; they cling desperately to their Confucian ethics so they will be thought of as civilized. And yet they enjoy nothing more than watching one of their own being sliced to ribbons, gaining the same cruel enjoyment as a child does killing a puppy. Given the power, they would happily decimate a city, creating mountains of breasts and bound feet severed from women. There can be no greater pleasure. But that power is denied them, and the next best thing is to watch the slaughter of pigs, sheep, and people to satisfy their craving. If even this is beyond their reach, at least they can vent their fury by subjecting their children to threats of a thousand cuts. (ibid.)

316. Respectable, ambitious, idealistic, self-serving, individualistic, robust, and mighty Xiangzi took part in untold numbers of burial processions but could not predict when he would bury himself, when he would lay this degenerate, selfish, hapless product of a sick society, this miserable ghost of individualism to rest. (ibid.)

***Ruined City: A Novel*, Jia Pingwa, trans. Howard Goldblatt, U. of Oklahoma Press, 2016**
317. One class of people is on the public weal, a life of leisure they proudly reveal.
    A second class uses the wealth of others, and enjoys the protection of powerful brothers.
    A third class contracts for large amounts, charging wasteful spending to expense accounts.
    A fourth class lives on profits from rents, sitting at home to count dollars and cents.
    A fifth class, the judges, whose courtrooms are used, profit from both accuser and accused.
    A sixth class wields a surgical blade, filling pockets with cash from their trade.
    A seventh class, actors on the stage, by comic routines make a tidy wage.
    An eighth class, propaganda shills, turns slogans and chants into cashable bills.
    A ninth class teaches in our schools, but where luxury is concerned are impoverished tools.
    Society's masters stand high on the tenth rung, earnestly studying the life of Lei Feng. (the old beggar) (5)

318. Humans, on the other hand, remain in a state of ignorance after birth, knowing only how to eat and drink; they go to school to learn, but by the time they know how to think, they are nearing the end of their lives. Those who come after them repeat the process, going to school to dispel the ignorance of their own age, which explains why humans never grow big and tall. The cow wanted to explain all this to humans, but unfortunately was unable to use human speech. Oftentimes humans cannot recall what happened in the past, and after something has taken place, they open their thread-bound books to read "How can there be such astonishing similarities in history!" They sigh. The cow had to laugh at the pitiable humans. (146)

319. What is laughable is that they suffer from heart, stomach, liver, and nerve problems in their square or round or trapezoid concrete structures within the confines of four city walls. Forever vigilant in regard to hygiene, they wear facemasks, produce soaps to wash their hands and feet, invent medicines and vaccines, brush their teeth, and put condoms over their male organs. And they seem to wonder what it is all about. Research is conducted, meetings are held, leading to the conclusion that the population must be reduced, so they promote the idea of a powerful bomb that will kill off everyone but their own families. (147)

320. Yes. As the ancients said, a wife cannot compare with a concubine, a concubine cannot compare with a prostitute, and a prostitute cannot compare with a secret lover. These days, nine out of ten couples manage to hang on to their marriage. But I'm just joking. Just joking. (the old man selling mirror cakes) (217)

321. They have a clever brain, but that brain is precisely the cause of their regression. The cow finally realized what a city really was: a place where regressed humans congregate after they can no longer adapt to nature and the universe, when they are afraid of the wind, the sun, the cold, and the heat. If a human were put on a vast prairie or on a high mountain cliff, he would not be the equal of a rabbit, even a ladybug. The cow's head hung even lower at these thoughts, and she heard a passerby say:
"Would you look at that old cow. What a stupid animal!"
The cow was not upset; she snorted, laughing at the man. (262)

322. "I know you hate me, Zhuang Laoshi." She hiked up her robe and sat down on a leather chair in front of the sofa. "You hate me because of Tang Wan'er. I admit I told Dajie everything, but it was partly because she beat me so savagely and partly because she was the one who found the message on the pigeon. She was suspicious when she read the note, and everything would have been fine if I'd kept quiet no matter how hard she hit me. But I didn't. I told her a lot of things. Now I want to explain to you why I did that. I was jealous of Wan'er. I was jealous because, like me, she had no city residency and had run away with Zhou Min, worse than anything I'd done, yet she'd managed to win your heart. I've been at your side all along, and yet—"
"Stop it, Liu Yue. She didn't win my heart. I was the one at fault. Don't you think I ruined her? Everything is over now."
"If that's what you think, then haven't you also ruined me? You're marrying me off to the mayor's son. Do you really think I can love him? I will have to close my eyes to marry him. It was you who changed Tang Wan'er and me into real women and gave us the courage and confidence

to start a new life. And in the end, it was you who ruined us. But in the process, you also ruined yourself, your image, and your reputation, along with Dajie and this family."

It finally dawned on Zhuang that this had been the root cause of his depression. (465)

323. Meng came to see him once, criticizing him for being cocooned so long in literary creation that he no longer knew how to live in society. He dealt with everything as if it were art, which was what had gradually put him in this state, and look where that had gotten him. Now did he plan to continue the way it was? "You worry that you can't let this one or that one go. But what about yourself? You're a celebrity, and a celebrity must live a more carefree and expansive life than others, while you, just look how you suffer."

Zhuang laughed silently, saying that Meng's ideas were alien to him. He hadn't agreed with Meng's opinions before, and he wouldn't agree with them now; all he wanted was for his friends to butt out. He said that Tang Wan'er was gone and Niu Yueqing had left home, which was a punishment from God. He and he alone would have to endure it. (491)

The Scholars, Wu Ching-tzu, trans. Yang Hsien-yi and Gladys Yang, Foreign Languages Press, 1964

324.   Men in their lives
         Go on different ways;
         Generals, statesmen,
         Saints and even immortals
         Begin as ordinary people.
         Dynasties rise and fall,
         Mornings change to evenings;
         Winds from the river
         Bring down old trees
         From a former reign;
         And fame, riches, rank
         May vanish without a trace.
         Then aspire not for these,
         Wasting your days;
         But drink and be merry,
         For who knows
         Where the waters carry the blossom
         Cast over them?

The idea expressed in this poem is the commonplace one that in human life riches, rank, success and fame are external things. Men will risk their lives in the search for them; yet once they have them within their grasp, the taste is no better than chewed tallow. But from ancient times till now, how many have accepted this? (ch. 1)

325. Kneeling, Fan Chin answered, "Yes, Your Excellency."
    "How old are you this year?"
    "I gave my age as thirty. Actually, I am fifty-four."
    "How many times have you taken the examination?"

"I first went in for it when I was twenty, and I have taken it over twenty times since then." (ch. 3)

326. "Now that you have become a gentleman," went on Butcher Hu, "you must do things in proper style. Of course, men in my profession are decent, high-class people; and I am your elder too—you mustn't put on any airs before me. But these peasants round here, dung-carriers and the like, are low people. If you greet them and treat them as equals, that will be a breach of etiquette and will make me lose face too. You're such an easy going, good-for-nothing fellow, I'm telling you this for your own good, so that you won't make a laughing-stock of yourself." (Fan's father-in-law) (ibid.)

327. Lying there at the point of death, Yen Ta-yu stretched out two fingers and refused to breathe his last; and when his nephews and servants made various wild guesses whether he meant two people, two events or two places, he simply shook his head.

But now his wife had stepped forward to say: "I'm the only one who understands you. You're worried because there are two wicks in the lamp—that's a waste of oil. If I take out one wick, it will be all right."

Suiting her actions to her words, she removed one wick. All eyes were fixed on Mr. Yen, who nodded his head, let fall his hand, and breathed his last. (ch. 6)

328. He was sitting at his counter one day when an old neighbour dropped in for a chat, and saw that though it was the tenth month Kai was still in a linen gown.

"My friend," he said, "I can see you are very hard up. You helped a great many people in the past, but none of them come here now. All your relatives are quite comfortably off; why don't you go to talk things over with them and borrow enough to set up a proper business, so that you can make a living?"

"Why, uncle," replied Kai Kuan, "don't you know the proverb? Warm feelings may turn to coldness. Men are drawn to prosperity but not to adversity." (ch. 55)

Selections from Records of the Historian, Szuma Chien, trans. Yang Hsien-yi and Gladys Yang, Foreign Languages Press, 1979

329. Another day he asked about government again and Confucius said, "The main thing is economy in the use of wealth."

The duke was pleased and would have given the field of Nihsi to Confucius as his fief had not Yen Ying protested, "These Confucians are such unruly windbags, so arrogant and self-willed that there is no controlling them. They set great store by long mourning and bankrupt themselves for a sumptuous funeral; it would never do if this became the custom. A beggar who roams the land talking is not a man to entrust with affairs of state. Ever since the passing of the great sages and the decline of the Chou Dynasty, the rites and music have fallen into decay. Now Confucius lays such stress on appearance and costume, elaborate etiquette and codes of behaviour that it would take generations to learn his rules—one lifetime would not be enough! To adopt his way of reforming the state would not be putting the common people first." ("Confucius," 4)

330. One day Confucius was playing the chimes when a man with a wicker crate passed the door and said, "Poor fellow, playing the chimes! He is self-willed but does not know himself. It is useless to talk with him." (13)

331. Then Fan Li left, sending Wen Chung a letter from Chi in which he said, "When all the birds are killed the good bow is put away. When the cunning hares are dead the hounds are made into stew. The king of Yueh with his long neck and predatory mouth is a good companion in time of trouble but not in time of peace. You had better leave."

After receiving this letter, Wen Chung stayed away from court on the pretext of illness but slanderers accused him of plotting rebellion. Then Kou-chien sent him a sword with this message, "You told me of seven ways to conquer Wu and by using three of them I have overthrown it. That leaves you with four—why not try them with my kingly ancestors?" Thereupon Wen Chung committed suicide. ("Kou-chien, King of Yueh," 53)

Serve the People!, Yan Lianke, trans. Julia Lovell, Black Cat, 2007

332. To contemporary eyes, life back then must seem lacking in emotional depth. More often than not, however, psychological complexity exists only in novels, as authors fill in details absent from protagonists' actual thoughts. As emotion, like comedy, is essentially immediate, its outward expressions tend to the superficial rather than the profound. (ch. 4)

333. As things stood, matters had now swung from the deadly serious to the unimaginably ridiculous—to a level of absurdity beyond Wu Dawang's own comprehension, but still artistically consistent with the fantastical parameters of our story. Neither character, in fact, had grasped the full ludicrousness of the scene they were acting out, or of their roles within it. Perhaps, in very particular circumstances, emotional truth can shine only through the curtain of farce, while earnest restraint will always fail to ring true. Maybe absurdity is the state that all affairs of the heart are, finally, destined for: the ultimate and only test of worth. (ch. 5)

"*Shunkouliu* (doggerel verse)," Helen Xiaoyan Wu, in *Encyclopedia of Contemporary Chinese Culture*, ed. Edward L. Davis, Routledge, 2005

334. *Shunkouliu* are anonymous doggerel verses. They are also called *minyao* or folk rhymes. They are especially of the topical and political types, and reflect ordinary people's opinions. To an extent, they are similar to political cartoons in the West. Numerous *shounkouliu* [*sic*] have been created to satirize corruption in an entertaining way. E.g.

> *Love and Don't Love*
>
> They don't love work but a dance floor.
> They don't love their good wives but their young mistresses.
> They don't love their thatched huts but villas.
> They don't love thrift but luxury. (pinyin transcription of the original omitted —Ed.)
>
> High-ranking cadres amuse themselves with men and women,
> Intermediate-ranking cadres are dishonest and immoral in their ways,
> Ordinary cadres have become by second nature hooligans. (ibid.)

335.   An official doesn't fear the hardship of drinking;
       And thinks nothing of endless cups and glasses.
       The steaming 'lover's hot pot' simmers;
       There're also seafood and barbecued fish balls.

Sauna and massage make him warm all over,
And he plays mahjong till it gets cold just before dawn.
What makes him happier is that the girl has snow-white skin;
He's all smiles after Ms Three Accompanies has done whatever he wanted.

. . . [The above] is especially popular as it is an imitation of Mao's poem, 'Long March', praising the Red Army which had endured extreme hardship. (ibid.)

"*Shunkouliu*: Popular Satirical Sayings and Popular Thought," Perry Link and Kate Zhou, in *Popular China: Unofficial Culture in a Globalizing Society*, ed. Perry Link, Richard P. Madsen, and Paul G. Pickowicz, Rowman and Littlefield, 2002
336. According to one, the "basic principles" of a Party member indeed numbered four:

My salary? Basically stored.
Liquor? I basically hoard.
My wife? Is basically bored. [Because I use other women.]
My job? Basically ignored. (99)

337. The following summary view of corruption seems to have been created by Beijing taxi drivers following the embezzlement trial of Beijing Mayor Chen Xitong in 1998:

If we don't root out corruption, the country will perish.
If we do root out corruption, the Party will perish.

(101)

The *Songs of the South: An Ancient Chinese Anthology of Poems by Qu Yuan and Other Poets*, trans. David Hawkes, Penguin, 1985
338. But the Fragrant One refused to examine my true feelings:
He lent ear instead to slander, and raged against me. ("*Li Sao* 'On Encountering Trouble,'" ll. 39–40)

339. All others press forward in greed and gluttony,
No surfeit satiating their demands:
Forgiving themselves, but harshly judging others;
Each fretting his heart away in envy and mal-ice. (ll. 57–60)

340. Truly this generation are cunning artificers,
From square and compass turn their eyes and change the true measurement,
Disregard the ruled line to follow their crooked fancies;
To emulate in flattery is their only rule. (ll. 89–92)

341. Zhòu cut up and salted the bodies of his ministers;
And so the days were numbered of the House of Yin. (ll. 159–60)

342. The world today is blinded with its own folly:
You cannot make people see the virtue inside you. (ll. 267–68)

343. You hate the deep and studious search for beauty,
But love a base knave's braggart blusterings;
And so the crowd press forward and each day advance in your favours,
And true beauty is forced far off, and retires to distant places. ("*Jiu zhang* 'Nine Pieces,'" III 'A Lament for Ying' (Ai Ying), ll. 57–60)

344. The world is turbulent and impure;
They call a cicada's wing heavy and a ton weight light;
The brazen bell is smashed and discarded; the earthen crock is thunderously sounded;
The slanderer struts proudly, the wise man lurks unknown.
Alas, I am silenced: who can know of my integrity?' ("*Bu ju* 'Divination,'" 205)

"Stale Mates," Zhang Ailing (Eileen Chang), in *The Longman Anthology of World Literature*, 2nd ed., v. F, ed. Djelal Kadir and Ursula K. Heise, Pearson/Longman, 2009
345. Both of his ex-wives were much richer than he was after the divorce settlements. But they never helped him out, no matter what straits he got into from providing for three women and their squabbling servants and later their children. He could not really blame them, taking everything into consideration. He would not have minded it so much if "That of the House of Fan" did not taunt him continually about the others' lack of feeling for him.

And now that he had lived down the scandal and ridicule, people envied him his *yan fu*, glamorous blessings—extraordinary in an age that was at least nominally monogamous, for it was already 1936—living with three wives in a rose-covered little house by the lake. On the rare occasions when he tried to tell somebody he was unhappy, the listener would guffaw. "Anyhow," the friend would say, "there are four of you—just right for a nice game of mahjong."

***Three Hundred Tang Poems*, trans. and ed. Peter Harris, Knopf, 2009**
346. There is a fine woman of peerless beauty
Living in seclusion in an empty valley.
She says she is from a good family, but one
That has fallen on hard times, relying on grass and trees.
When there was turmoil Within the Passes
Her brothers were all put to death—
What did it matter that they were high officials?
She could not retrieve their dead bodies.
The world feels distaste for decline and decay;
Its affairs all change like a flickering candle flame.
Her husband is a superficial fellow
And his new woman is as pretty as jade.
Even the mimosa knows to fold its leaves at dusk;
Mandarin ducks do not pass the night alone.
He only has eyes for the new woman's smiles—
No way for him to hear the old one crying. (Du Fu, "A fine woman," 45)

347. The source of the truth is not at all understood;
The world follows after false tracks. (Liu Zongyuan, "Paying an early-morning visit to the monastery of Master Chao to study Chan Buddhist sutras," 182)

348. In her cottage she knows nothing
     of elegant silks and scents;
She thinks of getting a go-between
     but that distresses her more.
Who will love a person of quality,
     somebody with talent?
Everyone falls for fashionable women
     made up in exotic ways.
She's prepared to vaunt the stitching skills
     she has in her ten fingers,
But not to compete at who is better
     at painting their eyebrows long.
She wields her needle and gold thread bitterly,
     year in and year out,
Making wedding costumes that
     are for other people to wear. (Qiu Taoyu, "A poor woman," 202)

349. And tell the girl next door her hopes can't rest
On imitating the lady's knitted brow! (Wang Wei, "Xi Shi," 219)

350. Her man is wealthy and well-placed,
     in the first flush of youth,
By temperament proud and spendthrift
     even more than the prodigal Ji Lun. ("Luoyang girl—a girl," 220)

351. Tax revenue officials have a royal mandate,
But they are comparable to raiders, are they not?
Nowadays these tax collectors are so oppressive
It's as if they are cooking people over a fire.
How can those that are paragons of our time
Be so by destroying people's lives? (Yuan Jie, "For my local officers on the retreat of raiders," 251)

***Three Kingdoms: A Historical Novel*, attributed to Luo Guanzhong, trans. Moss Roberts, U. of California Press/Foreign Languages Press, 1991**
352. On one such occasion, with all of officialdom present, several hundred enemy troops from the north who had voluntarily surrendered were brought in. Then and there Dong Zhuo ordered his guards to mutilate them: some had their limbs lopped off; some, their eyes gouged out; some, their tongues cut; some were boiled in vats. The howls of the victims shook the officials so that they could not hold their chopsticks. But Dong Zhuo kept drinking, chatting, and laughing away, utterly unperturbed, as was his wont. (ch. 8)

353. Now then, Dong Zhuo has an adopted son, Lü Bu, a man of extraordinary courage and might, but, like his stepfather, a slave to his passions. (ibid.)

354. Lu Su said to Zhou Yu, "Why do you want to see Xuande?" "He's the craftiest owl on earth," responded Zhou Yu. "I must be rid of him. This is my chance to lure him here and kill him, and save our house future grief." (ch. 45)

355. Beans asimmer on a beanstalk flame
From inside the pot expressed their ire:
"Alive we sprout on a single root—
What's your rush to cook us on the fire?" (Cao Zhi) (ch. 79)

The Three-Body Problem, Cixin Liu, trans. Ken Liu, Tor, 2016
356. "Take those frauds who practice pseudoscience—do you know who they're most afraid of?" (Wang)

"Scientists, of course." (Da Shi)

"No. Many of the best scientists can be fooled by pseudoscience and sometimes devote their lives to it. But pseudoscience is afraid of one particular type of people who are very hard to fool: stage magicians. In fact, many pseudoscientific hoaxes were exposed by stage magicians. Compared to the bookworms of the scientific world, your experience as a cop makes you far more likely to perceive such a large-scale conspiracy." (ch. 10)

357. Do you think I became famous for myself? To my eyes, the entire human race is a pile of garbage. Why would I care what they think? But if I'm not famous, how do I direct and channel their thinking? (Pan) (ch. 21)

358. Human society can no longer rely on its own power to solve its problems. It can also no longer rely on its own power to restrain its madness. Therefore, we ask our Lord to come to this world, and with Its power, forcefully watch over us and transform us, so as to create a brand-new, perfect human civilization. (Pan) (ibid.)

To Establish Peace: Being the Chronicle of the Later Han dynasty for the years 189 to 200 AD as recorded in Chapters 59 to 63 of the Zizhi tongjian of Sima Guang, Sima Guang, trans. Rafe de Crespigny, Internet ed., v. 2, openresearch-repository.anu.edu.au
359. Nonetheless, even as they swallowed one another those military leaders in provinces and commanderies still sought to justify themselves by reference to the honour of Han. (Sima Guang) (Jian'an 24: 219 A.D.)

The Travels of Lao Can, Liu E, trans. Yang Xianyi and Gladys Yang, Chinese Literature, 1983
360. The magistrate laughed and said, "Good. You have all suddenly become kind-hearted. You know how to be kind-hearted to Yu Xueli but will not be kind-hearted to your master; for whether he is guilty or not, if we release him he will not rest content, and I shall not be able to keep my post in future. The proverb says, 'When you cut grass you must pull out the roots,' and so it is here. This woman was even more odious, for she was obsessed with the idea that I had dealt unjustly

with her family. If she were not a woman, even though she is dead, I would give her another two thousand strokes to vent my anger." (Dong) (ch. 5)

361. It is said that Lao Can and Shen Dongchao were discussing the magistrate and how it was just because he was talented and wanted quick promotion that he committed so many acts of injustice; then they both sighed. (ch. 7)

***The Ugly Chinaman and the Crisis of Chinese Culture*, Bo Yang, trans. and ed. Don J. Cohn and Jing Qing, Allen & Unwin, 1992**

362. Neither the Greeks nor the Egyptians of today bear any relationship to their ancient fore-bears, while Chinese today are the direct descendants of the ancient Chinese. How have such a great people and nation degenerated into such ugliness? Not only have foreigners bullied us; what is worse, for centuries we've been tormented by our own kind from tyrannical emperors to despotic officials and ruthless mobs. ("The Ugly Chinaman," 7)

363. Why must Chinese people who have the guts to speak the truth suffer so terribly? I have asked a number of people from the mainland why they ended up in prison. Their answer was, 'Because I said a few things that happened to be true'. And that's the way it is. But why does telling the truth land one in such unfortunate circumstances? The way I see it, this is not a personal problem, but a fundamental flaw in Chinese culture. (8)

364. Chinese people are notorious for quarrelling and squabbling among themselves. (11)

365. Every culture flows on unceasingly like a great river. But as the centuries go by, cultures accumulate all sorts of flotsam and jetsam, such as dead fish, dead cats, and dead rats. When this detritus piles up on the river bed, the river ceases to flow and turns stagnant. The deeper the river, the thicker the layer of sludge; the older the river, the more thoroughly the sludge rots, until the river turns into one huge fermentation vat, a stinking repository of everything filthy and disgusting under the sun. ("The Chinese and the Soy Paste Vat," 39–40)

366. A wise man once said: 'He who knows something but does not act upon it does not possess true knowledge'. If you recognise the importance of co-operating with others, but don't co-operate with others yourself, then you don't recognise the importance of co-operation. This weakness is not inherent in the Chinese personality, but rather results from regularly overdosing on Confucian medicine and suffering from chronic indigestion. (from *Crashing into the Soy Paste Vat*, "Signs and Symptoms of Chinese Cultural Senility," 64)

367. On paper, China is a highly civilised country. In the flesh, however, Chinese people are barbarians. (from *The Comprehensive Mirror Marketplace*, "Signs and Symptoms of Chinese Cultural Senility," 76)

368. Chinatowns are infernal machines that swallow Chinese people alive. People working in Chinatowns illegally without US residence permits have little choice but to slave away in sweatshops where they barely earn enough to feed themselves. Like indentured servants they spend their entire lives in these factories, with no-one to complain to. But even if they had such a

sounding board, it is unlikely they would use it. Illegal sewing factories in Chinatown almost exclusively exploit Chinese people. (81–82)

369. The Chinese slave mentality manifests itself in ten ways:

1 Chinese people are addicted to shouting 'Long live So-and-so'.

2 Chinese people are superstitious by nature.

3 Chinese people respond uniformly to all tyrants, bullies and corrupt officials with a philosophy of resigned toleration.

4 The Chinese people cannot appreciate authentic democracy, so they make a fuss about 'slave democracy'.

5 Chinese people are cruel to their own kind, which perhaps explains their frequent infighting.

6 Chinese people excel at acting shrewdly and playing it safe.

7 Chinese people survive on hope. They do not control their own destinies and allow their lives to be run by tyrants and despots, so they have never learned to use their own brains to improve things. Rather they embrace the hope that despotic rulers will magically transform themselves into enlightened sovereigns, and that tyrannical officials will turn themselves into upright upholders of the law, and make life easy for them.

8 Chinese people are clinically and certifiably paranoid.

9 Chinese people are bound by all sorts of odd conventions and restrictions, many of which are old, ingrained habits.

10 Chinese people are chameleons. (Bo Ren, "Ten manifestations of the slave mentality," *Pai Hsing Semi-monthly* (Hong Kong), 1 April 1985, 129–34)

370. For years, whenever people talked about what is wrong with the Chinese people, the blame was always laid on foreign imperialists. But the last 30 years have demonstrated that the blame lies with our own soy paste vat culture. In fact if the soy paste vat culture hadn't created a nation of Ugly Chinamen, the foreign imperialists would never have got their foot in the door in the first place.

　　　The soy paste vat culture created despots and tyrants just as it created the slave mentality among the common folk. Tyranny and the slave mentality have caused untold catastrophes for China. (134)

***Vignettes from the Late Ch'ing: Bizarre Happenings Eyewitnessed over Two Decades*, Wu Wo-yao, [abr. and] trans. Shih Shun Liu, Chinese U. of Hong Kong Press, 1975**

371. This happened two years ago, when the Viceroy was mentally upset and worried. When he was young, he was addicted to sex. Now that he is advanced in age, he still has six or seven concubines of seventeen or eighteen, let alone a number of maidservants with whom he has illicit relations. He is so noted for his sexual desire that certain people tend to flatter him through this channel. (Chi-chih) (ch. 1)

372. This shows how careful you should be when coming into the world and making your friends. As a matter of fact, this man has not only stolen, but has engaged in gambling, swindling and kidnapping, and he would stop at nothing to benefit himself. He counts among his friends many worthless fellows roaming the rivers and lakes. Taking advantage of his official title, he has committed innumerable lawless acts. (ibid.) (ch. 2)

373. Upon further inquiry from me, he pulled out of his pocket a folder, which be handed to me. When I opened it, I saw a list of all the districts of Kiangsu written on it with a figure under each, ranging from 7,000 or 8,000 to 20,000 or 30,000 taels. I asked him to explain. Thereupon, Chi-chih left his seat of honour and took one of the side chairs, whispering to me, "This is a short cut to quick appointment. Once the prescribed amount is submitted, appointment is guaranteed within ten days. Of course the prices set are for permanent commissions, and those for provisional ones are lower." (ibid.)

374. Loving ostentation, a Manchu stops at nothing to show off, no matter how poor he may be. (ch. 3)

375. "There was once some talk," Chi-chih replied, "about raising the opium tax with a view to prohibition, but somehow nothing came of it. In my view prohibition in one or two provinces is ineffectual, and to produce results, the whole country must act under imperial orders."
    "That would be a difficult matter," I said.
    "Not really," Chi-chih continued, "because once the measure is approved, heavy taxes will be levied on opium-smokers, who will have to be registered. Those whose names are on the black list will not be permitted to take the state examinations or to become officials or open large commercial establishments. In that case opium-smokers will naturally disappear. Unfortunately nine out of ten of our present office-holders are afflicted with the addiction. Who would suggest a measure that would wipe them out?" (ch. 6)

376. This case illustrates the peril of official life, I'm afraid. The lady we have just seen is the widow of Chen Chung-mei [sic], a gentleman who successfully passed the imperial examination and who was given the title of Hsien Magistrate. He was a very capable man, but having been assigned to this province for more than ten years, he not only didn't have a chance to fill a single magistrate's vacancy, but failed even to hold more than a very few interim posts. Especially in recent years he was in great difficulty. For seven years he did not have a single job. He had to sell or pawn everything he had. A few days ago he was so desperate that he committed suicide by hanging himself. (Chi-chih) (ch. 7)

377. Showing the paper to me, he pointed to one item and commented, "What a mess there is in our country!" As I gazed at the paper, I saw the headline "Warship Sinks Itself." The news dispatch read:
    After sailing into Shanghai, the warship "Yu-yuan" made its way to Shihpu one day. Detecting a whiff of smoke on the horizon, the officers suspected that it was a French warship. Greatly frightened, the captain of the "Yu-yuan" sought to escape at full steam. Observing the extreme speed of the oncoming vessel, the captain was even more frightened. He opened the scuttle, sank the ship, dragged the crew out and sent them ashore in a sampan. A false report was made that on the sudden approach of an enemy vessel the "Yu-yuan" was hit and sunk. It is reported that the superior authorities are thoroughly investigating the matter and ordering the Shanghai *Taotai* [sic] to consult with the shipyard with a view to bringing the sunken vessel to the surface. (ibid.)

378. "Dear Auntie, please tell me," I pleaded, "what has happened in our home."

"Nothing in particular," said my aunt. "After several days of rain last month our clan shrine was hit by lightning, and it was decided that the corner of the house affected should be repaired. The head of our clan is your first grand-uncle, who suggested that the expenses should be shared by all our clansmen, a hundred taels being determined as your share. Your mother withheld her consent, saying that though our clan cannot lay claim to a large number of people, the repair is after all a minor one requiring not more than several hundred thousand cash and doesn't at all justify the amount of a hundred taels levied on us. We shouldn't have to pay so much even if we footed the entire bill.

"From then on there has been no end of trouble. In addition, there are other minor differences which cannot be explained in detail. Finally your mother could do nothing but declare that the matter could not be settled until your return. After this was made clear, there was peace for a few days, so your mother wrote you a letter, telling you not to come home. Unknown to us, you received the telegram you referred to. I suppose it must have been sent by those people to make you hurry home. That is why your mother said that you should not appear in public until our plans are made." (ch. 8)

379. "What did you mean when you referred to 'stealing'?" I asked when Hsiao-yun had left.

"Whatever is useful is stolen from the Bureau," Teh-chuan [sic] replied. "Externally every precaution is taken. At the door of the bureau an inspector is stationed and checks everything taken out. In fact, however, members of the staff are permitted at least to take home the so-called left-over coal, which has not been burned through, and which can be used for small stoves. This left-over coal is loaded into baskets, which can of course hold a lot of other things as well."

"In that case," I commented, "isn't everything stolen from the Bureau of Manufacture?" (ch. 14)

380. "Needless to say," Teh-chuan replied, "many things are just tricks. Let me give you one or two examples. Some priests treat diseases by drawing amulets instead of using drugs. . . .

"Also, the way the Taoists from Mao Shan thrust their hands into oil pans provides another example. Superficially it is very exciting to see one of them pick out copper coins one by one with their hands from an apparently boiling oil pan. As a matter of fact, however, the boiling effect comes from a foam which is formed by borax thrown into the oil. Under even slight heat the borax dissolves into a liquid, but before it does so, it forms a foam. It is the latter which gives the impression of boiling oil, but actually the oil is not very hot." (ch. 15)

381. "Having been unemployed for a long time, Ching-i was hard up and borrowed or pawned some of Hsi-chuan's [sic] personal belongings. Being a miser, Hsi-chuan could not tolerate this for long, and so the two brothers got along on bad terms. As a result, Ching-i reported to his father on Hsi-chuan's relations with Ah Liang, and in his letters be magnified the matter as much as he could. This elicited from the father an order that Hsi-chuan end his life and in addition an instruction to Ching-i to force his brother to commit suicide.

"As Hsi-chuan's neighbour, I've tried my best to mediate in the trouble. But Ching-i was set on getting the personal effects left by the old concubine of his father, so he had no consideration whatever for his brother. He even personally bought the opium and forced his brother to take it. No sooner had the latter breathed his last than Ching-i opened the trunks left by his father's concubine, only to find them filled with waste-paper, bricks, tiles and stones. It is said that Hsi-chuan had given everything to Ah Liang, but this could not be confirmed." [Tuan-fu]

After listening to this, I heaved a deep sigh. Somewhat later Ching-i returned, and I exchanged some words with him. Then I took my leave. Two days after that, Tuan-fu suddenly turned up and said to me, "This Ching-i is really a brute."

I hastened to ask what it was all about. "Shortly after Hsi-chuan's death," Tuan-fu replied, "he sold his sister-in-law."

"What!" I exclaimed. "Who to?"

"To a brothel!" was the answer. (ch. 16)

382. "People who are fond of bragging generally have a bad character," I said, "but I don't know whether this applies to Hsueh-yu."

"Not only those who are fond of bragging," Teh-chuan replied, "but the fine painters I have met all had a bad character." (ch. 18)

383. "That's fine," I said, "but why are you embarking on such a vast plan of expansion?"

"Coming from a business family," replied Chi-chih, "it is natural for me. However, having entered officialdom, I can't openly get mixed up in business. In the presence of strangers, I say that the business belongs to you. Please keep the truth from your colleagues." (ch. 20)

384. In the evening, I went out for a stroll, and happened to see a pigeon standing on the roof. Suddenly I thought of my rifle, and saw a chance to make use of it. I hastened back to the room to fetch it. I loaded it and fired at the bird just as it started to fly away. The bird seemed to hang in the air for a moment and then it fell to the ground. When I picked it up I was greatly surprised.

I saw that there was a piece of paper attached to the bird's tail, and in the paper was wrapped an officially sealed examination question! (ibid.)

385. An official called Kou Tsai lived not far from Chi-chih's house. This man had received one appointment after another. Most recently he had been commissioned as Director General of the Nanking Manufacturing Bureau, while serving concurrently as Director of the Preparatory Bureau and the Excise Bureau, two other remunerative posts. Enjoying all this distinction and good fortune, Kou Tsai frequented brothels on the Chin-huai [sic] River. Infatuated with one of the prostitutes, he took her as one of his concubines at a cost of two thousand taels.

Without letting his wife in on this secret, Kou Tsai rented another house for his concubine. His wife was a jealous and violent woman. She heard rumours of this new concubine but she could not take any action before she confirmed them. (ch. 21)

386. "It's often said," I commented, "that many cases are actually decided by the clerk, while the magistrate is a mere puppet."

"That depends on the magistrate," Chi-chih replied. "Of course it's quite true that a clerk can easily manipulate cases. If he can't do anything on one point, he can play a trick on another, and there's no limit to the leeway that he has. A magistrate can't possibly watch over all the details." (ch. 23)

387. I told Shu-nung what I had seen in the street. He said, "After roaming the river up and down for two years, you should have learned a great deal. Why are you still so ignorant? It's nothing for a man in uniform to take a couple of raviolas free of charge. You don't realize how greedy these

servicemen are. They richly deserve their nickname 'official robbers.' When such men are stationed anywhere, people in the neighbourhood can never rest. Vegetables in the fields, fish in the ponds, poultry let loose—they are all freely seized by these men, as if they were the public property of their battalion. Country women travelling back and forth are the objects of their flirtations, and who would dare to breathe a word of complaint?" (ch. 25)

388. This all happened last year. When I was home this time, my next-door neighbour received a letter from his son. What kind of business can you imagine she had in Singapore? It was a brothel! No sooner had they arrived in Singapore than the old woman forced her son's wife and concubine as well as the two maidservants to be prostitutes. At the same time she locked up her adopted son for two months and then sold him out to Kirin as a labourer. There he was placed under such strict discipline that he could not move freely even a single step. It was naturally only with great difficulty that he succeeded in writing a letter home. (Li-chih) (ch. 29)

389. "It makes me a little busier," Tung-hsien said, "but it pays to keep busy." Pointing to the table, he continued, "These are gifts a friend of mine is presenting to the Prime Minister. He has entrusted me with the presentation. I presume that he will get a handsome appointment in return."

On the table I saw two teak cases. When I opened the lids, I found that one of the cases contained fifty writing brushes and the other ten ink slabs, all of them made of solid gold, altogether weighing four hundred ounces. (ch. 35)

390. "As is well known," Tso-chih continued, "girls in Szechwan are the cheapest of all. In the provincial capital itself there are plenty of slave traders, who conduct their business in a teahouse specially opened by them for the purpose. A prospective purchaser goes to the teahouse, takes a seat there and has two bowls of tea served, one for himself and the other left on the table for no one in particular. The attendants will know at once that he is there for business. One of them will sit down with the customer and ask him how old a girl is desired. He will then take the customer to see the merchandise. When the choice is made and the price set, the transaction is sealed and the person or persons purchased will be delivered at his address. In general a girl aged from seven to eight costs eight or ten thousand cash; a virgin of sixteen or seventeen, forty or fifty thousand; and a married girl of the same age, about twenty thousand. (ch. 37)

391. The way was now clear for Kou to take his daughter-in-law to the Viceroy. After ending her mourning for her husband by bowing before his tablet, she changed into her new silk clothes and got into the sedan-chair. Soon she was carried to the Viceroy's yamen and handed over to him. (ch. 40)

392. "After Chi-chih learned of his mother's death," said Tzu-an, "he wired you and informed all his partners in all ports. Perhaps he should not have added in his letters that you happened to be away in Shantung. Thinking that both of you were no longer in charge, many of them began to be suspicious. Wu Tso-yu of Hankow was the first to tumble. He absconded with more than fifty thousand taels of the firm's funds. Incidentally a batch of drugs worth about ten thousand taels had been shipped downriver. Wu's questionable conduct became well known, so that those who could lay their hands on the drugs intercepted the shipment. At the same tune word was received by telegraph from various ports demanding the drugs. On one night alone eighteen telegrams were received, which drove Teh-chuan mad and immediately caused him to fall sick. Under the

circumstances I was forced to wire Peking and Tientsin to stop trading. In the meantime the Soochow and Hangchow branches had to close down. On that night one month's severance pay was distributed to the minor employees and depositors were handed their credit balances. Kuan Teh-chuan was so frightened that he did not even dare to go home but stayed with Wang Tuan-fu instead. I myself made Wen Shu-nung's house my temporary home." (ch. 44)

***Waiting for the Dawn: A Plan for the Prince: Huang Tsung-hsi's* Ming-i tai-fang lu, [trans.] Wm. Theodore de Bary, Columbia UP, 1993**

393. I have often wondered about Mencius' saying that "periods of order alternate with periods of disorder." How is it that since the Three Dynasties* there has been no order but only disorder? (*188n2: The Hsia, Shang, and Chou dynasties from earliest recorded times to 221 B.C.) (89)

394. In the beginning of human life each man lived for himself and looked to his own interests. There was such a thing as the common benefit, yet no one seems to have promoted it; and there was common harm, yet no one seems to have eliminated it. . . . To love ease and dislike strenuous labor has always been the natural inclination of man. (91)

395. Now the prince is master, and all-under-Heaven are tenants. That no one can find peace and happiness anywhere is all on account of the prince. In order to get whatever he wants, he maims and slaughters all-under-Heaven and breaks up their families—all for the aggrandizement of one man's fortune. Without the least feeling of pity, the prince says, "I'm just establishing an estate for my descendants." Yet when he has established it, the prince still extracts the very marrow from people's bones, and takes away their sons and daughters to serve his own debauchery. It seems entirely proper to him. It is, he says, the interest on his estate. Thus he who does the greatest harm in the world is none other than the prince. (92)

396. Until the end of the Three Dynasties there was Law. Since the Three Dynasties there has been no Law. (97)

397. Later rulers, once they had won the world, feared only that their dynasty's lifespan might not be long and that their descendants would be unable to preserve it. They set up laws in fear for what might happen, to prevent its coming to pass. However, what they called "Law" represented laws for the sake of one family and not laws for the sake of all-under-Heaven.

   The Ch'in abolished feudal fiefs and set up commanderies (*chün*) and prefectures (*hsien*) with the thought that this system would better serve their own interest. The Han gave domains to members of the royal house, thinking to have them stand as a buffer around their empire. The Sung abolished the regional commanderies because commanderies were not to their own advantage. Such being their laws and systems, how could they have manifested the slightest trace of consideration for all-under-Heaven? Indeed, could we call these "Law" at all? (97–98)

398. But after the prime ministership was abolished, the moment an emperor was succeeded by an unworthy son there was no worthy person at all to whom one could turn for help. Then how could even the idea of dynastic succession be maintained? (101–02)

399. Since the Three Dynasties right and wrong in the world have been determined entirely by the court. If the Son of Heaven favored such and such, everyone hastened to think it right. If he frowned upon such and such, everyone condemned it as wrong. The "keeping of public records and making of annual reports," state finances, military and judicial affairs—all have been left to petty subofficials. Rarely, indeed, has anyone escaped the evil tendencies of the times; consequently, people are apt to think the schools of no consequence in meeting the urgent needs of the day. Moreover, the so-called schools have merely joined in the mad scramble for office through the examination system, and students have allowed themselves to become infatuated with ideas of wealth and noble rank. Finally, because of the seductive influence of the court, there has been a complete change in the qualifications of schoolmen. Furthermore, those scholars with real ability and learning have often come from the countryside, having nothing to do with the schools from start to finish. So, in the end, the schools have failed even in the one function of training scholar-officials. (105)

400. Throughout the Han T'ang, and Sung dynasties there was an endless series of disasters brought on by eunuchs, but none of these was so frightful as the disasters of the Ming dynasty. During the Han, T'ang, and Sung, there were instances of eunuchs interfering with the government, but no instance of the government openly doing the bidding of eunuchs. In recent times the prime minister and the six ministries have been the nominal organs of administration. But the approval or disapproval of memorials has been determined first by private consultation and only then put into writing; the taxes collected in the empire have gone first of all to the palace storehouses and after this to the State Treasury of the Ministry of Revenue; penal matters have been handled first by the Eastern Yard and only after this by the law courts. There has been nothing in the government of which the same was not true. Consequently, the prime minister and six ministries have been nothing but functionaries carrying out the will of the eunuchs. (165)

401. When people had grown accustomed to such conduct over a long period of time, petty Confucians lost any understanding of high principles and fell in with this attitude, saying, "The Prince, our Father, is Heaven itself!" Therefore, when memorials were presented during the Ming, a man who knew quite well what was right and wrong, nevertheless did not dare to state dearly what was right and wrong. Instead he pointed out minor mistakes and ignored great errors, or concentrated his attention on modern usage and overlooked ancient precedent. He thought this the only proper way to serve his ruler. How was he to know that in these later times the character and thinking of men had been utterly reduced to servile depravity—all the work of eunuchs! Under such circumstances, what else can one expect but disastrous consequences? (167)

402. Having built themselves splendid palaces, there was nothing for it but to fill them with women. Having acquired so many women, there was nothing for it but to have eunuchs to guard them. One thing just followed another. (168)

***Xunzi: The Complete Text*, Xunzi, trans. Eric L. Hutton, Princeton UP, 2014**
403. Students in ancient times learned for their own sake, but the students of today learn for the sake of impressing others. ("An Exhortation to Learning," 5)

404. [H]e who flatters and toadies to me acts as a villain toward me. ("Cultivating Oneself," 9)

405. In the current era, there are people who ornament perverse doctrines and embellish vile teachings, such that they disturb and disorder the whole world. Their exaggerated, twisted, and overly subtle arguments cause all under Heaven to be muddled and not know wherein right and wrong and order and disorder are contained. ("Against the Twelve Master," 40)

406. Duke Huan of Qi was the most successful of the five hegemons, but among his early deeds he killed his elder brother and seized the state. In conducting internal family matters, there were seven of his sisters and aunts whom he did not marry off. Within his private chambers he indulged in extravagant entertainments and music. He was presented with the whole state of Qi as his portion, but he did not consider it sufficient. In foreign affairs, he deceived Zhu and ambushed Ju, and he annexed thirty-five states. Such was the impetuousness, corruption, perversion, and extravagance of his affairs and conduct. Simply how could he be worthy of praise in the school of the great gentleman! ("On Confucius," 47)

407. In most cases, the problem for people is that they become fixated on one twist and are deluded about the greater order of things. ("Undoing Fixation," 224)

408. Thus, among the cases of fixation, one can be fixated on desires, or one can be fixated on dislikes. One can be fixated on origins, or one can be fixated on ends. One can be fixated on what is far away, or one can be fixated on what is nearby. One can be fixated by broad learning, or one can be fixated by narrowness. One can be fixated on the ancient past, or one can be fixated on the present. In whatever respect the myriad things are different, they can become objects of fixation to the exclusion of each other. This is the common problem in the ways of the heart. (ibid.)

409. In past times, there were guest retainers who were fixated—such were the pernicious schools. Mozi was fixated on the useful and did not understand the value of good form. Song Xing was fixated on having few desires and did not understand the value of achieving their objects. Shen Dao was fixated on laws and did not understand the value of having worthy people. Shen Buhai was fixated on power and did not understand the value of having wise people. Huizi was fixated on wording and did not understand the value of what is substantial. Zhuangzi was fixated on the Heavenly and did not understand the value of the human. (226–27)

410. People's nature is bad. Their goodness is a matter of deliberate effort. Now people's nature is such that they are born with a fondness for profit in them. If they follow along with this, then struggle and contention will arise, and yielding and deference will perish therein. They are born with feelings of hate and dislike in them. If they follow along with these, then cruelty and villainy will arise, and loyalty and trustworthiness will perish therein. They are born with desires of the eyes and ears, a fondness for beautiful sights and sounds. If they follow along with these, then lasciviousness and chaos will arise, and ritual and *yi*, proper form and order, will perish therein. Thus, if people follow along with their inborn dispositions and obey their nature, they are sure to come to struggle and contention, turn to disrupting social divisions and order, and end up becoming violent. So, it is necessary to await the transforming influence of teachers and models and the guidance of ritual and *yi*, and only then will they come to yielding and deference, turn to proper form and order, and end up becoming controlled. ("Human Nature Is Bad," 248)

Zuo Tradition = Zuozhuan: Commentary on the "Spring and Autumn Annals," trans. Stephen Durrant, Wai-yee Li and David Schaberg, U. of Washington Press, 2016

411. The text says, "The Liege of Zheng overcame Duan at Yan." Gongshu Duan did not behave like a younger brother, so it does not speak of a younger brother. They were like two rulers, so it says "overcame." That it labels him "the Liege of Zheng" is to criticize his neglect of instruction: what happened is judged to have been Zheng's intention. That the text does not say he left Yan and fled is to express disapproval of him. (v. 1, "Lord Yin (722–712 BCE)," *Zuo*, 1.4b, 11)

412. In the second year, in winter, Lord Huan's wife, Lady Jiang, met with the Prince of Qi at Zhuo. This records an act of adultery. ("Lord Zhuang 2 (692 BCE)," *Zuo*, 2.1, 141)

413. The noble man said, "It says in the *Shang Documents*, 'The spread of iniquity is like the blazing of fire on grassland; since one cannot even approach it, how can one still beat it out?' Surely this fits Prince Ai of Cai!" ("Lord Zhuang 14 (680 BCE)," *Zuo*, 14.3, 175)

414. Renhao, the Liege of Qin, died. They took Yanxi, Zhonghang, and Qianhu, three sons of the Ziche lineage, and buried them with him. All were good men of Qin. The inhabitants of the capital grieved over them and composed in their honor the ode "The Oriole."

    The noble man said, "It is indeed fitting that Lord Mu of Qin did not become leader of the covenant. In death, he discarded his people. When the former kings departed from the world, they would leave behind proper norms. How could they ever take away the good men of the domain!" ("Lord Wen 6 (621 BCE)," *Zuo*, 6.3, 491)

415. On the eve of battle, Hua Yuan had slaughtered a sheep to feed his men, but his chariot driver Yang Zhen had been denied his portion. When it was time for battle, Yang said, "With yesterday's mutton, you were in charge, but in today's affair, I am in charge." He drove the chariot into the ranks of the Zheng army, hence Song's defeat. The noble man said of Yang Zhen: "He was not human. Because of a private grudge, he brought about defeat for the domain and devastation for the people. At that moment, what punishment could be too great for him? Where the *Odes* speaks of 'men of no goodness,' does it not refer to the likes of Yang Zhen! He inflicted harm on the people for his own satisfaction." ("Lord Xuan 2 (607 BCE)," *Zuo*, 2.1a, 589)

416. In autumn, the Red Di attacked Jin and reached Qing: this was because Xian Hu had summoned them.

In winter, the leaders of Jin chastised those responsible for the defeat at Bi and the military confrontation at Qing. They put the blame on Xian Hu, had him put to death, and completely extinguished his lineage. The noble man said, "'Evil came to him because he himself brought it on.' Would this not describe Xian Hu?" ("Lord Xuan 13 (596 BCE)," *Zuo*, 13.3–13.4, 669)

417. In the eighth month, Lord Wen of Song died. It was then that the extravagant burials began. The ashes of burnt clamshells and charcoal were used. The number of carriages and horses accompanying the dead were increased. For the first time humans were sacrificed to follow the deceased in death. The number of vessels and implements was multiplied. Four pillars supported the outer coffin, which had a roof in the palace style. The coffin was ornamented on three sides and on the top.

The noble man said of Hua Yuan and Yue Ju that "in this they did not behave as subjects should. A subject is one who brings order to chaos and removes confusion. That is why he braves death to fight for the right path. Now as for these two men, when the ruler was alive they abetted his desires, and when he died, they added to his extravagance. This amounted to abandoning the ruler to iniquities. How was this the proper behavior for a subject?" (v. 2, "Lord Cheng 2 (589 BCE)," *Zuo*, 2.4, 725)

418. The noble man said, "To count on one's insignificance and make no defensive preparations is the greatest of offenses; to be prepared even for the unexpected is the greatest good. Ju counted on its insignificance and did not repair its city walls, so that in the course of twelve days Chu vanquished its three major cities. Is this not because of the lack of defensive preparation?" ("Lord Cheng 9 (582 BCE)," *Zuo*, 9.10b, 783)

419. The noble man said, ". . . In an era of good government, noble men honor the capable and yield to those below them, while the common men labor to the utmost to serve those above them. That is why, above and below, there is ritual propriety, and the slanderous and iniquitous ones are banished afar. This comes about because they do not come into conflict, and this is called 'beautiful virtue.' When the polity falls into disorder, noble men call attention to their achievements in order to lord it over the common men, and the common men boast of their special skills in order to impose on noble men. That is why, above and below, there is no ritual propriety, and disorder and violence arise together. This comes about because they contend over their respective merits, and this is called 'obscured virtue.' The ruin of the domain and patrimony must always derive from this." ("Lord Xiang 13 (560 BCE)," *Zuo*, 13.3b, 1001)

420. The Prince of Chen went to Chu. Gongzi Huang complained about Qing Hu and Qing Yin at the Chu court, and the leaders of Chu summoned them. They had Qing Yue go to Ch u, and he was put to death. The Qing lineage used Chen as a base for revolt. In summer, Qu Jian went with the Prince of Chen and laid siege to Chen. The men of Chen fortified their city. The frame collapsed, and leaders of the Qing lineage put some workmen to death. The workmen passed orders to one another, and each group of men killed their respective chief, and then they killed Qing Hu and Qing Yin. The leaders of Chu restored Gongzi Huang to his domain. The noble man said that the Qing lineage was undutiful: its excesses could not be left unchecked. That is why it says in the *Documents*, "It is the Mandate that does not remain constant." ("Lord Xiang 23 (550 BCE)," *Zuo*, 23.2, 1105)

421. In the eighth year, in spring, a stone spoke in Weiyu, in Jin. The Prince of Jin asked the music master Kuang, "For what reason did the stone speak?"

He answered, "Stones cannot speak. They may be possessed by something, or if not, then the people may have misheard something. Yet the saying goes, 'When a person is not timely in attending to his affairs, grudges and enmities stir among the people, and mute things speak.' At present your palace is lofty and extravagant, but the strength of the people is exhausted. Grudges and enmity arise together, and no one can protect his livelihood. Is it not appropriate that a stone should speak?"

The Prince of Jin was building the Siqi Palace at this time. (*Zuo*, 8.1, 1437)

Appendix: Additional Sources

Authors' names (family name first without a comma) followed by their works are ordered alphabetically in pinyin. If a Chinese text is available online, a link is given (some texts in classical Chinese carry a *baihua* translation; many have annotations); if not, a WorldCat page link to the most libraries carrying the item is provided. (For older books, libraries typically have more than one edition or publisher.) The use of simplified or traditional characters varies with the source. An English translation, if available, is also given. (Multiple translations are only given for a few authors, Bai Juyi and Lu Xun in particular.) The time is that of writing or publication. The entries consist of what I've saved over the years as well as most of those introduced in sixteen histories of and reference works in Chinese literature I've consulted.

Along 阿垅 (1907–1967)

Nanjing xue ji 南京血祭, 1987: https://www.worldcat.org/title/nanjing-xue-ji/oclc/62610676&referer=brief_results.

Author unknown 作者不详

90 *niandai chuqi shunkouliu size* 90年代初期顺口溜四则, 1990s, online text: https://www.chazidian.com/xiaohua30280/.

90*hou* 80*hou* 70*hou* 60*hou* 50*hou de wunai* 90后80后70后60后和50后的无奈, 2000s, online text: https://blog.51cto.com/u_1033573/225360.

Butong niandai de butong kouhao, jingpi! 不同年代的不同口号, 精辟!, online text: https://bbs.wenxuecity.com/joke/555966.html.

Chao gaoxiao shunkouliu! Zhide shoucang!! 超搞笑顺口溜! 值得收藏!!, 2021, online text: https://www.toutiao.com/w/1711232328963080/.

Chaozuo 炒作, 2010, online text: http://m.poluoluo.com/bk/d5/201010/80164.html.

Dangdai minyao jijin 当代民谣集锦, n.d., online text: http://www.xys.org/xys/ebooks/literature/poetry/shunkouliu.txt (方舟子整理).

Dayoushi baitian xiang Jiao Yulu wanshang xiang Lei Zhenfu de quanwen 打油诗白天像焦裕禄晚上像雷振富的全文, 2013, online text: https://zhidao.baidu.com/question/513973063.html.

E'gao 恶搞, 2000s, videos: https://www.google.com/search?q=%E6%81%B6%E6%90%9E&source=lmns&tbm=vid&bih=7

13&biw=1448&rlz=1C5CHFA_enUS704US704&hl=en&sa=X&ved=2ahUKEwjMm6m3p5D5
AhXXsXIEHe2aD18Q_AUoAnoECAEQAg.

Fengci youmo 2012 nianzhong zongjie 讽刺幽默 2012年终总结, 2013, online text:
http://cn.epochtimes.com/gb/13/1/27/n3786583.htm. (For more from this site:
https://www.epochtimes.com/gb/tag/%E8%AE%BD%E5%88%BA%E5%B9%BD%E9%BB%9
8.html.

Gou yu lang de duihua 狗与狼的对话, 2014, online text:
http://www.360doc.com/content/14/0819/16/4593371_403106823.shtml.

Guanchang fengqing 官场风情, n.d., online text:
http://www.wcai.net/joke/guanchang.htm.

Guonei qishi bu nan hun zhiyao shede laolian shede wei—fanju li de maoni 国内其实不
难混 只要舍得老脸舍得胃—饭局里的猫腻, 2009, online text:
https://m.wenxuecity.com/myblog/14556/200908/18542.html.

Jiaoshou ba mian yao chun, sichu zhuanqian, yue lai yue xiang shangren 教授八面摇唇,
四处赚钱, 越来越像商人, http://blog.mzsky.com/u/4689/blog_30332 (scroll down; this post was
untitled; the title given is the beginning line).

Jinü wansui 妓女万岁, 2000, online text:
http://www.xys.org/forum/messages/30000/37585.html.
"Long Live Prostitutes," trans. John STAINLESS STEEL, 2004:
http://longliveprostitutes.blogspot.com/2004/06/long-live-prostitutes.html.

Lanren jiao duo, guanliao zhuyi hui duo 懒人觉多, 官僚主义会多, n.d., online text:
https://www.chazidian.com/xiaohua29421/. (Click 上一条 or 下一条 for more 顺口溜.)

Lingdao laile zenme ban?—xin minyao daquan 领导来了怎么办? —新民谣大全, 2005,
online text: http://45.35.85.74/news/gb/pubvp/2005/12/200512141945.shtml.

Nanren kan wan buxin ni bu duzi teng ...... 男人看完不信你不肚子疼 ......, 2010, online text: https://bbs.wenxuecity.com/joke/375159.html.

Nannü guanxi si da xin dongxiang 男女关系四大新动向, 2013, online text:
http://zzwav.com/thread-150750-1-1.html.

Nanren de zongjie—jingdian shunkouliu 男人的总结—经典顺口溜, 2008, online text:
https://blog.wenxuecity.com/myblog/37170/200807/26875.html.

Nü mishu zhen youcai: ba guanchang duilian shouji qiquanle 女秘书真有才: 把官场对联收集齐全了, 2014, online text:
https://blog.wenxuecity.com/myblog/59021/201407/15020.html.

Ren zhong hua 人中画, 1780, online text:
https://www.kekeshici.com/xiaoshuo/mingqing/65795.html.

Shaozhuang bu nuli, zhang da wan shouji 少壮不努力, 长大玩手机, 2014, online text:
http://0668gz.com/thread-27724-1-1.html.

Shidai minyao:Minyao shidai 时代民谣:民谣时代, 2007, online text:
https://m.hnbllw.com/zhihuirensheng/2019/0205/14728.html.

Shizheng ge 时政歌, 2011, online text:
http://www.360doc.com/content/11/1204/15/6017453_169593850.shtml.

Shunkouliu 顺口溜, n.d, online text: https://www.diyifanwen.com/tool/shunkouliu/ (40 pp.).

Shunkouliu>fengci shi>>wenzhang liebiao 顺口溜>讽刺诗>>文章列表, n.d., online text:
https://gdjyw.com/wap/humor/fcs/.

Wangluo yulu 网络语录, 2008, online text:
https://blog.wenxuecity.com/myblog/37767/200812/388.html.

Wanquan pilu 完全披露, n.d., online text:
https://baike.baidu.com/item/%E5%AE%8C%E5%85%A8%E6%8A%AB%E9%9C%B2/12780951.

Wenhua shidian 文化视点, n.d., online text:
https://luckynet.uzai.ca/xiaohua/shunkouliu/shp/165222.html (has link to 笑话大全).

Xiagang mei, bie liulei, tingxiong zoujin yezonghui 下岗妹, 别流泪, 挺胸走进夜总会, n.d., online text: http://bbs.cnhubei.com/blog-433919-7000.html.

Yanzi fu 燕子赋, 敦煌俗赋, Tang Dynasty, online text: https://zh.m.wikisource.org/zh-hans/%E9%B7%B0%E5%AD%90%E8%B3%A6.
"The Swallow and the Sparrow," trans. Arthur Waley, in *Ballads and Stories from Tun-Huang*, Routledge, 2005, 11–24.

Yemu jianglin hou, women de shehui shi zhege yangzi de 夜幕降临后, 我们的社会是这个样子的, n.d., online text: http://www.jokeji.cn/jokehtml/mj/20100304135545.htm.

Yiqian tidao jiehun, xiangdao "tianchangdijiu" 以前提到结婚, 想到"天长地久," 2000s, online text: https://weibo.com/5839513740/EpfXfz98d. (This post was untitled; the title given is the beginning line.)

You Zhongguo tese de naojin ji zhuanwan wenti 有中国特色的脑筋急转弯问题, 2011, online text: https://bbs.wenxuecity.com/bbs/netiq/133028.html.

Youguan qiang yan de duanzi 有关抢盐的段子, 2011, online text: https://bbs.wenxuecity.com/joke/385730.html.

Zhang de shuai you shenme yong? Kao Qinghua you shenme yong? Xue jingji you shenme yong? 长得帅有什么用？考清华有什么用？学经济有什么用?, 2010, online text: https://www.yantan.us/bbs/viewthread.php?tid=97215.

Zhanguo ce 战国策, Western Han (刘向编), online text: https://so.gushiwen.cn/guwen/book_53.aspx.
Chan-kuo ts'e, rev. ed., trans. and annot. with an intro. J.I. Crump, with an index by Sharon J. Fidler with J.I. Crump, Center for Chinese Studies, U. of Michigan, 1996.

Zhe shi shei bian de, tai TMD jingdianle ...... 这是谁编的,太TMD经典了......, 2011, online text: https://blog.wenxuecity.com/myblog/35254/201112/9319.html.

Zheng chu, fu chu, zuihou dou buzhi luo zai hechu ...... 正处, 副处, 最后都不知落在何处 ......, 2017, online text:
http://www.360doc.com/content/17/0721/06/45198195_672969910.shtml.

Zhenggong·Zui taiping 正宫·醉太平, Yuan Dynasty, online text: https://baike.baidu.com/item/%E6%AD%A3%E5%AE%AB%C2%B7%E9%86%89%E5%A4%AA%E5%B9%B3.

Zhongguo dangdai minyao jingdian quan bian 中国当代民谣经典全编, 2004, online text: http://www.chinaaffairs.org/gb/detail.asp?id=43773.

Zhongguo shehui xianzhuang zhi zongjie 中国社会现状之总结, 2010, online text: https://blog.wenxuecity.com/myblog/52312/201012/11748.html.

Bai Juyi 白居易 (772–846)
Qinzhongyin shi shou 秦中吟十首, Tang Dynasty, online text:
https://baike.baidu.com/item/%E7%A7%A6%E4%B8%AD%E5%90%9F%E5%8D%81%E9%A6%96/3876769?fromtitle=%E7%A7%A6%E4%B8%AD%E5%90%9F&fromid=53857.
"Songs of Chang'an (Ten Poems)," trans. Rewi Alley, in *Bai Juyi, 200 Selected Poems*, New World Press, 1983, 120–31. (Alley's anthology includes the original Chinese titles.)
For a translation of the 7th poem in the group, 轻肥, see quote no. 187 above under *Literatures of Asia*. For a translation of the last poem in the group, 买花, see the item below, *The Selected Poems of Po Chü-I*, 31. Hinton also has no. 7 on p. 30.

Xin yuefu 新乐府, Tang Dynasty, online text:
http://www.dushu369.com/shici/HTML/8120.html.
The Selected Poems of Po Chü-I, trans. David Hinton, New Directions, 1999 (7 poems, 18–27).

Other translations of Bai Juyi's satirical and other poems can be found in *Poetry and Prose of the Tang and Song*, trans. Yang Xianyi and Gladys Yang, Panda Books, 1984, 109–34; *Po Chü-I: Selected Poems*, trans. Burton Watson, Columbia UP, 2000; *Waiting for the Moon: Poems of Bo Juyi*, trans. with an intro. Arthur Waley, foreword by Craig R. Smith, Axios Press, 2012; 许渊冲英译白居易诗选 *Selected Poems of Bai Juyi*, 许渊冲英译, 许渊冲赏析, 中国对外翻译出版有限公司, 2014 and *Translations from Po Chü-i's Collected Works*, trans. and descr. Howard S. Levy, Paragon Book Reprint Corp., 1971, v. 1 (he calls the two groups of poems "didactic").

Cai Yong 蔡邕 (133–192)
Shu xing fu 述行赋, Eastern Han, online text:
https://so.gushiwen.cn/shiwenv_8c171067659b.aspx.
"*Fù* Recounting a Journey," in *A Significant Season: Cai Yong (ca. 133–192) and His Contemporaries*, Mark Laurent Asselin, American Oriental Society, 2010, 302–28.

Can Xue 残雪 (1953–)
Gongniu 公牛, 1985, online text: https://www.99csw.com/book/259/11043.htm.

Wuxiang jie 五香街, 2002, online text: https://m.ddxsss.com/book/78936/list.html.
Five Spice Street, trans. Karen Gernant and Chen Zeping, Yale UP, 2009 (titled 突围表演 in 1988).

Cao Qujing 曹去晶 (Qing Dynasty)
Gu wang yan 姑妄言, 1730, online text: https://ctext.org/wiki.pl?if=gb&res=190138.

Cao Yu 曹禺 (1910–1996)
Beijingren 北京人, 1941, online text: http://www.5156edu.com/html/25732/1.html.

Chen Baichen 陈白尘 (1908–1994)
Jiehun jinxingqu 结婚进行曲, 1942: https://www.worldcat.org/title/jie-hun-jin-xing-qu/oclc/301810333&referer=brief_results.

Luanshi nannü 乱世男女, 1939: https://www.worldcat.org/title/luan-shi-nan-nu-san-mu-xi-ju/oclc/950930140&referer=brief_results.

Shengguan tu 升官图, 1946: https://www.worldcat.org/title/sheng-guan-tu-san-mu-qi-chang-hua-ju/oclc/17036328&referer=brief_results.

Suihan tu 岁寒图, 1945: https://www.worldcat.org/title/sui-han-tu/oclc/301500866&referer=brief_results.

Chen Cun 陈村 (1954–)

Sishi hushuo 四十胡说, 1996: https://www.worldcat.org/title/si-shi-hu-shuo/oclc/35214096&referer=brief_results.

Chen Jian'gong 陈建功 (1949–)

Quanmao 鬈毛, 1986, online text: https://yd.qq.com/web/reader/b7d327607275fe75b7dace1k9bf32f301f9bf31c7ff0a60. "Curly Locks," *Chinese Literature*, Summer 1988, 47–128.

Chen Jiying 陳紀瀅 (1908–1997)

Di cun zhuan 荻村傳, 1951: https://www.worldcat.org/title/di-cun-zhuan/oclc/18029147&referer=brief_results.
Fool in the Reeds, 4th ed., trans. and adapted Eileen Chang, Rainbow Press, 1961.

Chen Ruoxi 陳若曦 (1938–)

The Short Stories of Chen Ruoxi, Translated from the Original Chinese: A Writer at the Crossroads, ed. Hsin-sheng C. Kao, Mellen, 1992 (contains 路口, 15–76).

Yin xianzhang 尹縣長, 1976: https://www.worldcat.org/title/yin-xian-chang/oclc/1154702903&referer=brief_results.
The Execution of Mayor Yin and Other Stories from the Great Proletarian Cultural Revolution, rev. ed., ed. Howard Goldblatt, trans. Nancy Ing and Howard Goldblatt, Indiana UP, 2004.

Chen Siyi 陈四益 (文) (1939–)

Huitu shuang bai yu 绘图双百喻, 丁聪画, 1997: https://www.worldcat.org/title/hui-tu-shuang-bai-yu/oclc/373559054&referer=brief_results.

Shixiang xiezhen tu 世相写真图, 丁聪画, 2001: https://www.worldcat.org/title/shi-xiang-xie-zhen-tu/oclc/50134851&referer=brief_results.

Chen Yingzhen 陳映真 (1937–2016)

Tang Qian de xiju 唐倩的喜劇, 2001: https://www.worldcat.org/title/tang-qian-de-xi-ju/oclc/49694236&referer=brief_results.

Chen Yuanlong 陳元龍 (1652–1736)

Fengyu 諷喻, 欽定四庫全書 御定歷代賦彙外集卷十六, 陳元龍奉敕編, Qing Dynasty, online text: https://www.kanripo.org/text/KR4h0139/159#1a (22 pieces by 宋玉, et al., unpunctuated).

Chen Zizhan 陈子展 (1898–1990)

Chen Zizhan wen cun 陈子展文存, 2018: https://www.worldcat.org/title/chen-zizhan-wen-cun/oclc/1096269031&referer=brief_results, 2 vols.

Chi Bei'ou 池北偶/谭文瑞 (1922–2014)

Shitai wanxiang: Chi Beiou zixuan fengci shi sanbai shou 世态万象: 池北偶自选讽刺诗三百首, 2007: https://www.worldcat.org/title/shi-tai-wan-xiang-chi-bei-ou-zi-xuan-feng-ci-shi-san-bai-shou/oclc/1159553977&referer=brief_results.

Chi Li 池莉 (1957–)

Ni yiwei ni shi shei 你以为你是谁, 1995, online text: https://www.xyyuedu.com/writer/chili/niyiweinishishui/index.html.

Chimeiwangliang 魑魅魍魉 (unknown)

Mo Yan men de "gushi" 莫言们的"故事," 2012: https://www.zhihu.com/question/398259517 (scroll down).

Dai Qixiao 戴其晓 (编著) (1957–)

Dangdai zuixin liuxing shunkouliu daquan 当代最新流行顺口溜大全, 2010: https://www.worldcat.org/title/dang-dai-zui-xin-liu-xing-shun-kou-liu-da-quan/oclc/885799828&referer=brief_results.

Ding Ling 丁玲 (1904–1986)

San-Ba jie yougan 三八节有感, 1942, online text: https://www.zhonghuadiancang.com/wenxueyishu/10925/216017.html.

Wo zai Xia cun de shihou 我在霞村的时候, 1941, online text: https://www.99csw.com/article/5111.htm.
"When I Was in Xia Village," trans. Gary J. Bjorge, in *The Columbia Anthology of Modern Chinese Literature*, ed. Joseph S.M. Lau and Howard Goldblatt, Columbia UP, 1995, 143–58.

Zai yiyuan zhong shi 在医院中时, 1941, online text: https://www.zhonghuadiancang.com/wenxueyishu/10841/ (changed to 在医院中 in 1942).
"A Translation of Ting Ling's 'In the Hospital' and 'Thoughts on March Eighth'," Susan M. Vacca, Radcliffe College, 1976.

Ding Xilin 丁西林 (1893–1974)

Deng taitai huilai de shihou 等太太回来的时候, 1946: https://www.worldcat.org/title/deng-tai-tai-hui-lai-de-shi-hou/oclc/301979866&referer=brief_results.

Xilin dumuju 西林独幕劇, 1992: https://www.worldcat.org/title/xilin-du-mu-ju/oclc/222371537&referer=brief_results.

William Dolby (unknown) (comp. and trans.)

Chinese Humour: An Anthology, Carreg Publishers, 2005, 2 vols (chronological).

Dong Jieyuan 董解元 (active 1189–1208)

Xixiang ji zhugongdiao 西厢记诸宫调, Jin Dynasty, online text:
https://www.zhonghuadiancang.com/shicixiqu/xixiangjizhugongdiao/.
Master Tung's Western Chamber Romance = Tung Hsi-hsiang chu-kung-tiao: A Chinese Chante-fable, trans. Li-li Ch'en, Cambridge UP, 1976.

Dong Yue 董說 (1620–1686)

Xiyou bu 西遊補, 1841, online text: https://www.99csw.com/book/5121/index.htm.
The Tower of Myriad Mirrors: A Supplement to Journey to the West, 2nd ed., trans. Shuen-fu Lin and Larry J. Schulz, Center for Chinese Studies, U. of Michigan, 2000.

Dongfang Shanba 东方善霸 (pseudonym) (unknown)

Choulou de xueshuren 丑陋的学术人, 1999: https://www.worldcat.org/title/chou-lou-de-xue-shu-ren-choulou-de-xueshuren/oclc/682375993&referer=brief_results.

Feng Menglong 冯梦龙 (1574–1646)

Xiao fu 笑府, Ming Dynasty, online text:
https://ctext.org/wiki.pl?if=gb&res=318400&remap=gb.
Feng Menglong's Treasury of Laughs: A Seventeenth-Century Anthology of Traditional Chinese Humour, Hsu Pi-ching, Brill, 2015 (bilingual).

For more collections of jokes, see https://www.zhonghuadiancang.com/tags-73-0.html.

Feng Naichao 馮乃超 (1901–1983)

Xianzhang 县长, 1986, in 馮乃超文集: https://www.worldcat.org/title/feng-nai-chao-wen-chi/oclc/227724149&referer=brief_results, v. 1, 267–87.

Feng Weimin 冯惟敏 (1511–1578)

Haifu shantang cigao 海浮山堂词稿, 凌景埏,谢伯阳点校, Ming Dynasty:
https://www.worldcat.org/title/hai-fu-shan-tang-ci-gao/oclc/1112273777&referer=brief_results.

Feng Xuefeng 冯雪峰 (1903–1976)

Kua de rizi 跨的日子, 1947: https://www.worldcat.org/title/kua-de-ri-zi/oclc/51016641&referer=brief_results.

Gao Qiwo 高启沃, Zang Weixi 藏维熙 (both unknown) (选注)

Lidai fenyu sanwen xuan 历代讽谕散文选, 1983: https://www.worldcat.org/title/li-dai-feng-yu-san-wen-xuan/oclc/885516295&referer=brief_results.

Gao Xiaosheng 高晓声 (1928–1999)

Chen Huansheng shang cheng, 陈奂生上城, 1980, online text:
http://www.5156edu.com/page/09-02-05/42830.html.
"Chen Huansheng Goes to Town," in *A Knife in Clear Water and Other Stories*, Shi Shuqing and others, trans. Vivian H. Zhang, Long River Press, 2012, 195–211.

Li Shunda zaowu 李顺大造屋, 1979, online text: https://www.99csw.com/book/2626/79821.htm.

"Li Shunda Builds a House," trans. Madelyn Ross, in *A Place of One's Own: Stories of Self in China, Taiwan, Hong Kong, and Singapore*, ed. Kwok-kan Tam, Terry S.H. Yip, Wimal Dissanayake, Oxford UP, 1999, 3–27.

Qingtian zai shang 青天在上, 1991: https://www.worldcat.org/title/qing-tian-zai-shang/oclc/25322524&referer=brief_results.

Gong Zizhen 龚自珍 (1792–1841)

Bing mei guan ji 病梅馆记, Qing Dynasty, online text: https://baike.baidu.com/item/%E7%97%85%E6%A2%85%E9%A6%86%E8%AE%B0/668369?fr=aladdin.

"My Plum Tree Infirmary," trans. 可可英语, http://www.kekenet.com/kouyi/201405/294864.shtml (bilingual).

Guo Dayu 郭大宇 (1948–), Xi Zhigan 习志淦 (unknown)

Xu Jiujing shengguan ji: Jingju 徐九经升官记: 京剧, 1982: https://www.worldcat.org/title/xu-jiujing-sheng-guan-ji-jing-ju/oclc/28245254&referer=brief_results (京剧《徐九经升官记》选段–当官难: https://www.youtube.com/watch?v=h8625BcWP4g.)

Ha Gong 哈公 (1933–1987)

Ha Gong guailun 哈公怪論, 1986: https://www.worldcat.org/title/ha-gong-guai-lun/oclc/23336649&referer=brief_results.

"Four Essays by Ha Gong," trans. Don J. Cohn, in *Renditions*, nos. 29 & 30, 1988, 320–27, online pdf: https://www.cuhk.edu.hk/rct/pdf/e_outputs/b2930/v29&30P320.pdf.

Ha Gong yulu 哈公语录, 1981: https://www.worldcat.org/title/hagong-yu-lu/oclc/57290584&referer=brief_results.

Han Han 韩寒 (in dispute) (1982–)

Sanchong men 三重门, 2000, online text: http://www.dushu369.com/zhongguomingzhu/scm/.

This Generation, ed. and trans. Allan H. Barr, Simon & Schuster, 2012 (blogs).

Han Shaogong 韩少功 (1953–)

Ba Ba Ba 爸爸爸, 1985, online text: https://www.99csw.com/book/2603/index.htm.

"Pa Pa Pa," in *Homecoming? and Other Stories*, trans. Martha Cheung, Research Centre for Translations, Chinese U. of Hong Kong, 1992, 35–90.

Han Yu 韩愈 (768–824)

Gui Pengcheng 歸彭城, Tang Dynasty, online text: https://zh.m.wikisource.org/wiki/%E6%AD%B8%E5%BD%AD%E5%9F%8E.

"Returning to P'eng-ch'eng [Hsü-chou]," trans. Stephen Owen, in *The Poetry of Meng Chiao and Han Yü*, Yale UP, 1975, 80–81.

Hui bian 讳辩, Tang Dynasty, online text:
https://baike.baidu.com/item/%E8%AE%B3%E8%BE%A9.
Kuhan 苦寒, Tang Dynasty, online text:
https://baike.baidu.com/item/%E8%8B%A6%E5%AF%92/23412388.
"Suffering from the Cold," trans. Stephen Owen, in *The Poetry of Meng Chiao and Han Yü*, Yale UP, 1975, 213–15.

Mao Ying zhuan 毛颖传, Tang Dynasty, online text:
https://baike.baidu.com/item/%E6%AF%9B%E9%A2%96%E4%BC%A0.
"Biography of Mao Ying," trans. James R. Hightower, in "Han Yu as Humorist," *Harvard Journal of Asiatic Studies*, 44.1, 1984, 10–14.

He Jingming 何景明 (1483–1521)
Dongmeng fu 东门赋, Ming Dynasty, online text:
https://baike.baidu.com/item/%E4%B8%9C%E9%97%A8%E8%B5%8B/13959741.

Huang Can 黄灿, Li Hongyi 黎洪溢 (both unknown) (选析)
Dangdai fengci shi 当代讽刺诗, 1990: https://www.worldcat.org/title/dang-dai-feng-ci-shi/oclc/756897504&referer=brief_results.

Huang Chunming 黄春明 (1935–)
Huang Chunming dianying xiaoshuo ji 黃春明電影小說集, 1989:
https://www.worldcat.org/title/huang-chun-ming-dian-ying-xiao-shuo-ji/oclc/813736377&referer=brief_results.

Shayonala, zaijian 莎喲娜啦·再見, 2009: https://www.worldcat.org/title/shayonala-zai-jian/oclc/429169881?referer=di&ht=edition.

The Taste of Apples, trans. Howard Goldblatt, Columbia UP, 2001. (Includes translations of eight of the stories in the two collections above. Earlier printings of 莎喲娜啦·再見 have fewer stories, so the translator must have gotten some of the stories elsewhere.)

Huang Fan 黃凡 (1950–)
Fandui zhe 反对者, 1984: https://www.worldcat.org/title/fan-dui-zhe/oclc/502209332&referer=brief_results.

Lai Suo 賴索, 1980: https://www.worldcat.org/title/lai-suo/oclc/76972352&referer=brief_results (title story).
"Lai Suo," in *Zero and Other Fictions*, ed. and trans. John Balcom, Columbia UP, 2011, 1–28.

Shangxin cheng 傷心城, 1983: https://www.worldcat.org/title/shang-xin-cheng/oclc/818508134&referer=brief_results.

Huang Wenxiong 黄文雄 (1938–)

Huang Wenxiong (zuojia), Weiji yulu, ziyou de mingren mingyan lu 黄文雄 (作家), 维基语录, 自由的名人名言录, online text: https://zh.wikiquote.org/wiki/%E9%BB%83%E6%96%87%E9%9B%84_(%E4%BD%9C%E5%AE%B6).

Huang Xingzeng 黄省曾 (1490–1540)

Qian fu 钱赋, Ming Dynasty, online text: https://zh.wikisource.org/zh-hans/%E6%AC%BD%E5%AE%9A%E5%8F%A4%E4%BB%8A%E5%9C%96%E6%9B%B8%E9%9B%86%E6%88%90/%E7%B6%93%E6%BF%9F%E5%BD%99%E7%B7%A8/%E9%A3%9F%E8%B2%A8%E5%85%B8/%E7%AC%AC358%E5%8D%B7 (scroll down).

She bing fu 射病赋, Ming Dynasty, in 历代赋鉴赏辞典: https://www.worldcat.org/title/li-dai-fu-jian-shang-ci-dian/oclc/1057707452&referer=brief_results, 898–902 (including annotations and appreciation).

Huang Zunxian 黄遵宪 (1848–1905)

Renjinglu shi cao 人境庐诗草, Qing Dynasty, online text: https://ctext.org/wiki.pl?if=gb&res=191731&remap=gb.
Within the Human Realm: The Poetry of Huang Zunxian, 1848–1905, J.D. Schmidt, Cambridge UP, 1994, pt. 3.

Huayangsanren 华阳散人 (ca. 1610–ca. 1675)

Yuanyang zhen 鸳鸯针, c. 1644/1645: https://www.worldcat.org/title/yuan-yang-zhen/oclc/1082534991&referer=brief_results.

Ji Yun 纪昀 (1724–1805)

Yuewei caotang biji 阅微草堂笔记, Qing Dynasty, online text: http://www.dushu369.com/gudianmingzhu/ywctbj/.
Shadows in a Chinese Landscape: The Notes of a Confucian Scholar, ed. and trans. David L. Keenan, M.E. Sharpe, 1999. (Another version was edited and translated by David E. Pollard.)

Jia Pingwa 贾平凹 (1952–)

Shanzhen yedian 山镇野店, 1981, in 贾平凹小说新作集: https://www.worldcat.org/title/jia-pingao-xiao-shuo-xin-zuo-ji/oclc/122768484&referer=brief_results, 244–54.

Jia Yi 贾谊 (200 B.C.–168 B.C.)

Jia Yi xin shu 贾谊新书 (or simply 新书), Western Han, online text: http://m.sbkk8.com/gudai/jiayixinshu/.
For a list of translations of five pieces, see "Jia Yi," in *Classical Chinese Writers of the Pre-Tang Period*, ed. Curtis Dean Smith, Gale Cengage, 2011, 78.

For more lists of translations, see "Jia Yi 賈誼 (ca. 200–168 b.c.e., var. 201–169 b.c.e.), also known as Jia sheng 賈生 (Scholar Jia)," in *Ancient and Early Medieval Chinese Literature: A Reference Guide*, pt. 1, ed. David R. Knechtges and Taiping Chang, Brill, 2010, 422–25.

Jiang Gui 姜貴 (1908–1980)

Xuanfeng 旋风, 1959: https://www.worldcat.org/title/xuan-feng/oclc/956552443&referer=brief_results.

Jin Shijie 金士杰 (1951–)

He zhu xin pei 荷珠新配, 1980: https://www.youtube.com/watch?v=vkjG_Dq7Q5Q (performance).

Jinmusanren 金木散人 (unknown)

Guzhang juechen 鼓掌绝尘, 1631, online text: https://read.lmeee.com/reader/3xf3ij.

Kang Hai 康海 (1475–1540)

Zhongshan lang 中山狼, Ming Dynasty: https://www.worldcat.org/title/zhong-shan-lang/oclc/1017067808&referer=brief_results.

Lai He 賴和 (1894–1943)

Dou nao re 鬥鬧熱, 1926, online text: https://zh.m.wikisource.org/wiki/%E9%AC%A5%E9%AC%A7%E7%86%B1.

Reshi 惹事, 1932, online text: https://zh.m.wikisource.org/wiki/%E6%83%B9%E4%BA%8B.

Yi gan cheng zai 一桿稱仔, 1926, online text: https://zh.m.wikisource.org/zh/%E4%B8%80%E6%A1%BF%E7%A8%B1%E4%BB%94.

All his works are online: https://zh.m.wikisource.org/zh/Author:%E8%B3%B4%E5%92%8C.

Lao She 老舍 (1899–1966)

Can Wu 殘霧, 1940, online text: http://www.bwsk.com/mj/l/laoshe/cw/index.html.

Chaguan 茶馆, 1957, online text: http://www.dushu369.com/zhongguomingzhu/chaguan/. *Teahouse: A Play in Three Acts*, trans. John Howard-Gibbon, Foreign Languages Press, 1980.

Er Ma 二马, 1929, online text: https://www.ppzuowen.com/book/laoshezuopinji/erma/. *Mr. Ma & Son: A Sojourn in London*, trans. Julie Jimmerson, Foreign Languages Press, 2004.

Lao Zhang de zhexue 老张的哲学 1926, online text: https://www.kanunu8.com/book3/8024/.

Lihun 离婚, 1933, online text:
https://yuedu.163.com/source/63a42c3a4789479e8dbca83899dff5d5_4.

Mao cheng ji 猫城记, 1932–33, online text: https://www.99csw.com/article/9119.htm.
Cat Country: A Satirical Novel of China in the 1930's by Lao She, trans. William A. Lyell, Jr.,
Ohio State UP, 1970.

Niu Tianci zhuan 牛天赐传, 1936, online text: https://www.kanunu8.com/book3/8027/.

Zhaozi yue 赵子曰, 1927, online text: https://www.dushu.com/showbook/129169/.

Li Boyuan 李伯元 (1867–1906)
Nanting si hua 南亭四話, Qing Dynasty: https://www.worldcat.org/title/nanting-sihua/oclc/1073388553&referer=brief_results.

Wenming xiaoshi 文明小史, 1906, online text:
https://www.feiku6.com/book/wenmingxiaoshi.html.
Modern Times: A Brief History of Enlightenment, trans. Douglas Lancashire, Chinese UP, 1996.

Li Er 李洱 (1966–)
Huaqiang 花腔, 2002: https://www.worldcat.org/title/hua-qiang-coloratura/oclc/1245255998&referer=brief_results.
Coloratura, trans. Jeremy Tiang, U. of Oklahoma Press, 2019.

Shiliu shu shang jie Yingtao 石榴树上结樱桃, 2004, online text:
https://weread.qq.com/web/reader/519324c07220757f519e529.

Li Guowen 李国文 (1930–)
Zhongguo wenren de linglei miankong 中国文人的另類面孔, 2009:
https://www.worldcat.org/title/zhongguo-wenren-de-linglei-miankong/oclc/730064036&referer=brief_results

Li Guoxiu 李国修 (1955–2013)
San ren xing bu xing 三人行不行, 1987: https://www.worldcat.org/title/li-guoxiu-xi-ju-zuo-pin-ji-collected-plays-of-hugh-ks-lee/oclc/861618046&referer=brief_results (v. 5 of his collected plays).

Shamuleitei 莎姆雷特, 1992: https://www.worldcat.org/title/li-guoxiu-xi-ju-zuo-pin-ji-collected-plays-of-hugh-ks-lee/oclc/861618046&referer=brief_results (v. 2 of his collected plays).

Li Jianwu 李健吾 (1906–1982)
Liang Yunda 梁允達, 1934: https://www.worldcat.org/title/liang-yunda/oclc/989104853&referer=brief_results.

Li Jie 李玠 (unknown) (编著)

Laobaixing de zhihui: Dalu dangdai shunkouliu shangxi 老百姓的智慧: 大陸當代順口溜賞析, 1998: https://www.worldcat.org/oclc/1291222211&referer=brief_results (contains 660 *shunkouliu*).

Li Jieren 李劼人 (1891–1962)

Li Jieren quanji 李劼人全集, 2011: https://www.worldcat.org/title/li-jieren-quan-ji/oclc/1240462638&referer=brief_results (v. 6. 中短篇小说).

Li Mengyang 李梦阳 (1472–1529)

Yi fu 疑赋, Ming Dynasty, online text: https://baike.baidu.com/item/%E7%96%91%E8%B5%8B/22687976?fr=aladdin.

Li Rui 李銳 (1949–)

"Electing a Thief," trans. Jeffery G. Kinkley, in *Furrows: Peasants, Intellectuals, and the State: Stories and Histories from Modern China*, comp. and ed. with an intro. Helen F. Siu, Stanford UP, 1990, 207–11.

Li Yu 李渔 (1611–1680?)

Rou putuan 肉蒲团, 1657, online text: https://www.tianshuge.com/gudianxiaoshuo/rouputuan/.
The Carnal Prayer Mat = Rou putuan, trans. with an intro. and notes Patrick Hanan, Ballantine, 1990.

Li Zongwu 李宗吾 (1879–1943)

Hou hei xue 厚黑学, 1911, online text: https://www.sto.cx/book-157378-1.html.
"*Thick Black Theory* 厚黑學: Annotated Translation," trans. Gino LaPaglia, in *The Cultural Roots of Strategic Intelligence*, Gino LaPaglia, Lexington, 2020, ch. 8 (translation of the original article).

Li Zongwu quanji 李宗吾全集, 2012: https://www.worldcat.org/title/li-zongwu-quan-ji/oclc/851540470&referer=brief_results, 2 vols.

Liang Xiaosheng 梁晓声 (1949–)

Fucheng 浮城, 1992, online text: https://b.guidaye.com/changxiao/9951/.

Hongyun 红晕, 2001, online text: https://weread.qq.com/web/bookDetail/bcd329907200baeabcd0b2b.

'Jiusan duanxiang: shei shi choulou de zhongguoren '九三断想: 谁是丑陋的中国人, 1995: https://www.worldcat.org/oclc/1286655053&referer=brief_results.

Minmie 泯灭, 1994, online text: https://www.99csw.com/book/2408/index.htm.

Panic and Deaf: Two Modern Satires, trans. Chan Hanming, ed. James O. Belcher, U. of Hawai'i Press, 2001.

Weiba 尾巴, 1996, online text: https://www.99csw.com/book/2409/index.htm.

Lin Yutang 林语堂 (1895–1976)

Lun zhengzhi bing 论政治病, 1933, online text: http://www.aisixiang.com/data/82820.html.

With Love and Irony, illus. Kurt Wiese, J. Day, 1940.

Ling Mengchu 凌蒙初 (1580–1644)

Er ke pai'an jingqi 二刻拍案惊奇, 1632, online text: http://www.dushu369.com/gudianmingzhu/ekqajq/.
Amazing Tales: Second Series, trans. Li Ziliang, Higher Education Press, 2006, 4 vols.

Pai'an jingqi 拍案惊奇, 1628, online text: http://www.dushu369.com/gudianmingzhu/ckpajq/.
Slapping the Table in Amazement: A Ming Dynasty Story Collection, trans. Shuhui Yang, Yunqin Yang, U. of Washington Press, 2018.

Ling Shuhua 凌叔华 (1900–1990)

Xiu zhen 绣枕, 1925, online text: https://www.99csw.com/article/2826.htm
"Embroidered Pillows," trans. Jane Parish Yang, in *Modern Chinese Stories and Novellas 1919–1949*, ed. Joseph S. M. Lau, C. T. Hsia, and Leo Ou-fan Lee, Columbia UP, 1981, 197–99.

Zhongqiu wan 中秋晚, 1928, online pdf: https://www.cuhk.edu.hk/rct/pdf/e_outputs/b04/v04p154.pdf (scroll down).
"The Night of Midautumn Festival," trans. Nathan K. Mao, in *Modern Chinese Stories and Novellas 1919–1949*, ed. Joseph S. M. Lau, C. T. Hsia, and Leo Ou-fan Lee, Columbia UP, 1981, 200–05.

Liu Binyan 刘宾雁 (1925–2005)

Ben bao neibu xiaoxi 本报内部消息, 1956, online text: http://www.liubinyan.com/selectedworks/Intranews.htm.
"Inside News," trans. Bennett Lee, in *Fragrant Weeds: Chinese Short Stories Once Labelled as "Poisonous Weeds,"* Liu Binyan and others, trans. Geremie Barmé and Bennett Lee, and ed. W.J.F. Jenner, Joint Pub., 1983, 1–70.

Zai qiaoliang gongdi shang 在桥梁工地上, 1956, online text: http://www.liubinyan.com/selectedworks/bridgesite.htm.

Liu Binyan 刘宾雁 (1925–2005) and Others

Fragrant Weeds: Chinese Short Stories Once Labelled as "Poisonous Weeds," trans. Geremie Barmé and Bennett Lee, and ed. W.J.F. Jenner, Joint Pub., 1983 (stories by Liu Binyan, Wang Meng, Qin Zhaoyang, Liu Shahe, Nan Ding, Liu Shaotang, Geng Longxiang, Li Guowen, Zong Pu).

Liu Ji 刘基 (1311–1375)

Fa jisheng fu 伐寄生赋, end of Yuan–beginning of Ming, online text: https://baike.baidu.com/item/%E4%BC%90%E5%AF%84%E7%94%9F%E8%B5%8B/2268795 9?fr=aladdin.

Liu Shahe 流沙河 (1931–2019)

Caomu pian 草木篇, 1957, online text: https://www.pinshiwen.com/gsdq/zwms/20190624125298.html.

Liu Xiang 刘向 (77 B.C.–6 B.C.)

Shuo yuan 说苑, Western Han, online text: http://gx.httpcn.com/book/824073d31f2545609c5e10f404ad2d5f/.
Garden of Eloquence, Shuoyuan, trans. and intro. Eric Henry, U. of Washington Press, 2022 (bilingual).

Xin xu 新序, Western Han, in 新序今註今譯: https://www.worldcat.org/title/xin-xu-jin-zhu-jin-yi/oclc/63061089&referer=brief_results.

Liu Xinwu 刘心武 (1942–)

Hei qiang 黑墙, 1982, online text: http://www.millionbook.com/xd/l/liuxinwu/000/017.htm.
"Black Walls," trans. Geremie Barmé, in *Black Walls and Other Stories*, ed. Don J. Cohn with an intro. by Geremie Barmé, Research Centre for Translation, Chinese U. of Hong Kong, 1990, 1– 13.

Liu Yuxi 刘禹锡 (772–842)

Yuanhe shinian zi Langzhou chengzhao zhi jing xizeng kanhua zhu junzi 元和十年自朗州承召至京戏赠看花诸君子, Tang Dynasty, online text: https://www.pinshiwen.com/gsdq/zwms/20190624125274.html
"Presented to and Mocking Those Flower-Viewing Noblemen in the Eleventh Year of the Yuanhe Reign after Being Summoned Back from Langzhou," trans. Wolfgang Kubin and William H. Nienhause, Jr., in "Liu Yuxi 劉禹錫," *Biographical Dictionary of Tang Dynasty Literati*, ed. William H. Nienhauser, Jr., assoc. ed. Michael E. Naparstek, Indiana UP, 2022, 229 (bilingual).

Zai you xuan dou guan 再游玄都观, Tang Dynasty, online text: http://www.dushu369.com/shici/HTML/8383.html.

"Visiting Xuandu Temple Again," trans. Wolfgang Kubin and William H. Nienhause, Jr., in "Liu Yuxi 劉禹錫," *Biographical Dictionary of Tang Dynasty Literati*, ed. William H. Nienhauser, Jr., assoc. ed. Michael E. Naparstek, Indiana UP, 2022, 230 (bilingual).

Liu Zhenyun 刘震云 (1958–)

Chigua shidai de ernümen 吃瓜时代的儿女们, 2017: https://www.worldcat.org/title/chi-gua-shi-dai-de-er-nu-men/oclc/1041103441&referer=brief_results.
Strange Bedfellows, trans. Howard Goldblatt and Sylvia Li-chun Lin, Cambria, 2021.

The Corridors of Power, Chinese Literature Press, 1994 (4 stories).

Guxiang mian he huaduo 故乡面和花朵, 1998, online text: https://weread.qq.com/web/bookDetail/c38323f0813ab6baag0113bc (scroll down).

Guxiang tianxia Huanghua 故乡天下黄花, 1991, online text: https://weread.qq.com/web/bookDetail/52932f305e43b1529c61868 (scroll down).

Guxiang xiangchu liuchuan 故乡相处流传, 1993, online text: https://weread.qq.com/web/bookDetail/42832ff05e43b0428d9e71a (scroll down).

Shouji 手机, 2003, online text：https://weread.qq.com/web/bookReview/list?bookId=ad632ba0527f77ad689c631 (scroll down).
Cell Phone: A novel, trans. Howard Goldblatt, MerwinAsia, 2011.

Wo bushi Pan Jinlian 我不是潘金莲, 2012, online text: https://weread.qq.com/web/bookDetail/0f732c405e43b40f717c2a4 (scroll down).
I Did Not Kill My Husband, trans. Howard Goldblatt and Sylvia Li-chun Lin, Arcade, 2014.

Wo jiao Liu Yuejin 我叫刘跃进, 2007, online text: https://weread.qq.com/web/bookDetail/27232c605e43ad272b67a70 (scroll down).
The Cook, the Crook, and the Real Estate Tycoon: A Novel of Contemporary China, trans. Howard Goldblatt and Sylvia Li-chun Lin, Arcade, 2015.

Yiqiang feihua 一腔废话, 2002, online text: https://www.99csw.com/book/2400/index.htm.

Yirisanqiu 一日三秋, 2021, online text: https://weread.qq.com/web/bookDetail/d0632c2072672b91d060472 (scroll down).

Liu Zhi 刘致 (?–between 1335 and 1338)

Duanzhenghao·Shang gao jian si 端正好·上高监司, Yuan Dynasty, online text: https://baike.baidu.com/item/%E7%AB%AF%E6%AD%A3%E5%A5%BD%C2%B7%E4%B8%8A%E9%AB%98%E7%9B%91%E5%8F%B8/7716565.

Liu Zongyuan 柳宗元 (773–819)

Ai ni wen 哀溺文, Tang Dynasty, online text:
https://www.mlbaikew.com/lsrw/wenyanwenyuedu/96163.html.

Ma shi chong wen bing xu 骂尸虫文并序, Tang Dynasty, online text:
http://61.134.53.202:81/refbook/detail.aspx?recid=R2006080610000112&db=CRFD.

Pi shuo 罴说, Tang Dynasty, online text:
https://www.gushimi.org/wenyanwen/3888.html.
"The Bear," in *Poetry and Prose of the Tang and Song*, trans. Yang Xianyi and Gladys Yang,
Panda Books, 1984, 144–45.

San jie (*bing xu*) 三戒 (并序), Tang Dynasty, online text:
http://www.dushu369.com/gudianmingzhu/HTML/41821.html.

Lu Bao 魯褒 (fl. late 3rd c.–early 4th c.)

Qian shen lun 钱神论, Western Jin, online text: https://zh.m.wikisource.org/zh-
hans/%E9%8C%A2%E7%A5%9E%E8%AB%96.
"On the Money God," trans. Victor Cunrui Xiong, in *Hawai'i Reader in Traditional Chinese
Culture*, ed. Victor H. Mair, Nancy S. Steinhardt, and Paul R. Goldin, U. of Hawai'i Press, 2005,
256–59.

Lu Guimeng 陆龟蒙 (?–881)

Lize congshu 笠泽丛书, Tang Dynasty, online text:
https://www.zhonghuadiancang.com/leishuwenji/11253/ (unpunctuated).
Robin D. S. Yates translates three of Lu's poems in *Sunflower Splendor: Three Thousand Years
of Chinese Poetry*, ed. Wu-Chi Liu and Irving Yucheng Lo, Indiana UP, 1975, including "A Lone
Wild Goose," 256–57.

William H. Nienhauser translates several *shi* and one *fu* by Lu in *P'i Jih-hsiu*, Twayne, 1979, 70–
71, 89–90, 106–07 and 112.

Lu Sidao 盧思道 (531–582)

Lao sheng lun 勞生論, Northern Qi–Sui Dynasty, online text:
https://zh.m.wikisource.org/zh-hant/%E5%8B%9E%E7%94%9F%E8%AB%96.

Lu Wenfu 陆文夫 (1928–2005)

Weiqiang 围墙, 1983, in 陆文夫小说选 = *Selected Stories by Lu Wenfu*, trans. Rosie A.
Roberts, 中國文學出版社 : 外语教学与研究出版社, 1999, 52–121 (bilingual).

Lu Xun 鲁迅 (1881–1936)

All his works are online:
https://weread.qq.com/web/search/books?author=%E9%B2%81%E8%BF%85.

For English translations, see
https://www.worldcat.org/search?q=kw%3AEnglish+au%3A%E9%B2%81%E8%BF%85&qt=advanced&dblist=638 and the following pages.

For a recent translation of his short stories, see *The Real Story of Ah-Q and Other Tales of China: The Complete Fiction of Lu Xun*, trans. Julia Lovell, Penguin, 2009.

For a four-volume translation of his works, see *Selected Works of Lu Hsun*, trans. Yang Xianyi and Gladys Yang, Foreign Languages Press, 1956–60: https://www.worldcat.org/title/selected-works-of-lu-hsun/oclc/324851&referer=brief_results.

Lu Yan 鲁彦 (1901–1944)
Huangjin 黄金, 1983: https://www.worldcat.org/oclc/1300884788&referer=brief_results.

Youzi 柚子, 1926, online text:
https://weread.qq.com/web/bookDetail/77132bf0813ab695fg01422e (scroll down).

Lu Yunzhong 卢允中 (unknown) (编选, 英译)
Zhongguo youmo gushi xuan: Han Ying duizhao 中国幽默故事选: 汉英对照, 周晓宇白话文翻译, 2007: https://www.worldcat.org/title/zhong-guo-you-mo-gu-shi-xuan/oclc/419266679&referer=brief_results.

Luo Yin 罗隐 (833–910)
Chan shu 谗书, Tang Dynasty , online text:
https://www.zhonghuadiancang.com/leishuwenji/chanshu/.
"Selections from 'Slanderous Writings,'" trans. Yang Xianyi, in *Chinese Literature*, Feb. 1982, 119–22 (7 selections).

Jiayi ji 甲乙集, Tang Dynasty, in *Luo Yin ji* 羅隱集, 雍文華校輯, 1983:
https://www.worldcat.org/title/luo-yin-ji/oclc/1196051692&referer=brief_results, 1–189.

Sunflower Splendor: Three Thousand Years of Chinese Poetry, ed. Wu-Chi Liu and Irving Yucheng Lo, Indiana UP, 1975, has three of his poems, including "Sent to the Ch'an Master Wu-hsiang," trans. Geoffrey R. Waters, 267.

Xue 雪, Tang Dynasty, online text:
https://baike.baidu.com/item/%E9%9B%AA/13350106.
"Snow," trans. Edward H. Schafer, in "Luo Yin 羅隱," *Biographical Dictionary of Tang Dynasty Literati*, ed. William H. Nienhauser, Jr., assoc. ed. Michael E. Naparstek, Indiana UP, 2022, 270 (bilingual).

Luofusanke 罗浮散客 (unknown)
Tian couqiao 天凑巧, Ming Dynasty, online text:
https://www.ckxxbz.com/book/tiancuqiao/.

Luopodaoren 落魄道人 (unknown)

Changyandao 常言道, Qing Dynasty, online text: http://quanben-xiaoshuo.com/n/changyandao/.

Ma Jian 馬健 (1953–)

Beijing zhiwuren 北京植物人, 2009: https://www.worldcat.org/oclc/1298650029&referer=brief_results.
Beijing Coma, trans. Flora Drew, Farrar, Straus and Giroux, 2008.

Lamian zhe 拉麵者, 2002: https://www.worldcat.org/title/la-mian-zhe-ma-jiangang-chang-pian-xiao-shuo-jing-xuan/oclc/801005499&referer=brief_results.
The Noodle Maker, trans. Flora Drew, Farrar, Straus and Giroux, 2005.

Zhongguo meng 中國夢, 2020: https://www.worldcat.org/title/zhongguo-meng-china-dream-ma-jian/oclc/1155370112&referer=brief_results.
China Dream, trans. Flora Drew, Chatto & Windus, 2018.

Ma Nancun/Deng Tuo 马南邨/邓拓 (1912–1966)

Yanshan yehua 燕山夜话, 1961, online text: http://www.dushu369.com/zhongguomingzhu/ysyh/.

Ma Qingwen 马清文 (1927–) (编著)

Qiaopihua daquan 俏皮话大全, 2010: https://www.worldcat.org/title/qiao-pi-hua-da-quan/oclc/886093809&referer=brief_results.

Ma Zhiyuan 马致远 (1250?–1324?)

Shuahaier·Jie ma 耍孩儿·借马, Yuan Dynasty, online text: https://baike.baidu.com/item/%E8%80%8D%E5%AD%A9%E5%84%BF%C2%B7%E5%80%9F%E9%A9%AC.

Mao Dun 茅盾 (1896–1981)

Qingming qianhou 清明前后, 1949: https://www.worldcat.org/title/qing-ming-qian-hou/oclc/298765446&referer=brief_results.

Meng Jinghui 孟京辉 (1964–)

Meng Jinghui xianfeng xiju dang'an 孟京辉先锋戏剧档案, 2010.
I Love XXX: and Other Plays, ed. Claire Conceison, Seagull, 2017.

Xianfeng xiju dang'an 先锋戏剧档案, ed. Meng, 2000: https://www.worldcat.org/title/xian-feng-xi-ju-dang-an/oclc/1183079362&referer=brief_results.

Mo Yan 莫言 (1955–)

Hong gaoliang jiazu 红高粱家族, 1988, online text:

http://www.dushu369.com/zhongguomingzhu/myzpj/hgljz/.
Red Sorghum: A Novel of China, trans. Howard Goldblatt, Viking, 1993.

Shengsi pilao 生死疲劳, 2006, online text:
https://www.99csw.com/book/2501/index.htm.
Life and Death Are Wearing Me Out: A Novel, trans. Howard Goldblatt, Arcade, 2008.

Tiantang suantai zhi ge, 天堂蒜薹之歌, 1988, online text:
http://www.dushu369.com/zhongguomingzhu/myzpj/ttstzg/.
The Garlic Ballads, trans. Howard Goldblatt, Viking, 1995.

Mu Shiying 穆时英 (1912–1940)

Mu Shiying: China's Lost Modernist, Andrew David Field, Hong Kong UP, 2014 (6 stories).

"Pierrot," 1930s, online text: http://www.millionbook.com/xd/m/mushiying/001/001.htm.

Ng Kim Chew 黄锦树 (1967–)

Slow Boat to China and Other Stories, trans. and ed. Carlos Rojas, Columbia UP, 2016.

Nie Gannu 聂绀弩 (1903–1986)

Nie Gannu zawen ji 聂绀弩杂文集, 1981: https://www.worldcat.org/title/nie-gan-nu-za-wen-ji/oclc/885534900&referer=brief_results.

Xueshu 血書, 1949: https://www.worldcat.org/title/xue-shu/oclc/869785361&referer=brief_results.

Nie Ren 聂仁 (unknown)

Minyao xia de zhongguo: Zhongguo dangdai shunkouliu shangxi 民谣下的中国: 中国当代顺口溜赏析, 2001: https://www.worldcat.org/title/min-yao-xia-de-zhong-guo-zhong-guo-dang-dai-shun-kou-liu-shang-xi/oclc/768668862&referer=brief_results.

Ouyang Yuqian 欧阳予倩 (1889–1962)

Zhongguo xiandai dumuju xuan 中國現代獨幕劇選, 1970?:
https://www.worldcat.org/title/zhongguo-xian-dai-du-mu-ju-xuan/oclc/48592601&referer=brief_results.

Pi Rixiu 皮日休 (ca. 834–ca. 883)

Pizi wen sou 皮子文藪, Tang Dynasty, 蕭滌非, 鄭慶篤整理, 2017:
https://www.worldcat.org/title/pi-zi-wen-sou/oclc/1004816322&referer=brief_results.

William H. Nienhauser, Jr., translates nearly forty poems and fifteen prose pieces by Pi in his biography, *P'i Jih-hsiu*, Twayne, 1979 (the finding list of translations is on pp. 151–52).

For a smaller collection, see *Sunflower Splendor: Three Thousand Years of Chinese Poetry*, ed. Wu-Chi Liu and Irving Yucheng Lo, Indiana UP, 1975, 259–66.

Pu Songling 蒲松龄 (1640–1715)
Liaozhai zhi yi 聊斋志异, 1766, online text: https://www.haoshuya.com/9/2528/.
Strange Tales from the Liaozhai Studio, trans. Zhang Qingnian, Zhang Ciyun, Yang Yi, People's China Pub. House, 1997, 3 vols.

Qiao Ji/Jifu 乔吉/乔吉甫 (1280–1345)
Shanpoyang·Dongri xie huai 山坡羊·冬日写怀, Yuan Dynasty, online text: https://so.gushiwen.cn/shiwenv_d5c8861f0fbc.aspx
"Tune: Sheep on the Slope·Thoughts in Winter (I)," trans. Xu Yuanchong, in *300 Yuan Songs = Yuanqu sanbai shou*, Haitun chubanshe, 2013, 89.

Qin Mu 秦牧 (1919–1992)
Qin Mu zawen 秦牧杂文, 1947: https://www.worldcat.org/title/qin-mu-za-wen/oclc/1290587003&referer=brief_results.

Qiu Huadong 邱华栋 (1969–)
Qiu Huadong jingxuan ji 邱华栋精选集, 2014: https://www.worldcat.org/title/qiu-hua-dong-jing-xuan-ji/oclc/953293720&referer=brief_results.

Qu Baiyin 瞿白音 (1909–1979)
Nanxia lieche: Dumuju ji 南下列車: 獨幕劇集, 1984: https://www.worldcat.org/title/nan-xia-lie-che-du-mu-ju-ji/oclc/320397037&referer=brief_results.

Ren Ximin 任喜民 (unknown)
Wenge xiaoliao daquan 文革笑料大全, 1993: https://www.worldcat.org/title/wen-ge-xiao-liao-da-quan/oclc/32137849&referer=brief_results.

Ruan Ji 阮籍 (210–263)
The Poetry of Ruan Ji and Xi Kang, trans. Stephen Owen and Wendy Swartz, ed. Xiaofei Tian and Ding Xiang Warner, De Gruyter, 2017 (bilingual, open-source).

Ruan Wenda 阮文達 (unkown)
Ruan shi chunqiu 阮氏春秋, 1967: https://www.worldcat.org/title/ruan-shi-chun-qiu/oclc/23319425?referer=di&ht=edition.

Sha Ting 沙汀 (1904–1992)
Huanxiang ji 還鄉記, 1948: https://www.worldcat.org/title/huan-xiang-ji/oclc/24420779&referer=brief_results.

Kunshou ji 困獸記, 1945: https://www.worldcat.org/title/kun-shou-ji/oclc/681091360&referer=brief_results.

Taojin ji 淘金記, 1943, online text: https://www.dushu.com/showbook/125274/.
Zai Qixiangju chaguan li 在其香居茶馆里, 1940, online text: https://www.pinshiwen.com/yuexie/wxjx/20190729160949.html.

Shang Yingshi 尚英時 (unknown) (编注)
Qiaopihua jingxuan 俏皮話精選, 1977: https://www.worldcat.org/title/qiao-pi-hua-jing-xuan/oclc/818435589&referer=brief_results.

Shanghai wenyi chubanshe 上海文艺出版社 (编)
Chong fang de xianhua 重放的鲜花, 1979: https://www.worldcat.org/title/chong-fang-de-xian-hua/oclc/880290386&referer=brief_results.

Shao Yanxiang 邵燕祥 (1933–)
Qie buke bawang "hao huangdi": Shao Yanxiang zawen zixuan ji 切不可巴望"好皇帝": 邵燕祥杂文自选集, 2015: https://www.worldcat.org/title/qie-bu-ke-ba-wang-hao-huang-di-shao-yan-xiang-za-wen-zi-xuan-ji/oclc/951392833&referer=brief_results.

For more titles in the series, 中国当代杂文精品大系, see https://www.worldcat.org/search?q=se%3A%22Zhong+guo+dang+dai+za+wen+jing+pin+da+xi.%22&fq=&dblist=638&qt=first_page.

You le bai pian 忧乐百篇, 1986: https://www.worldcat.org/title/you-le-bai-pian/oclc/1097250367&referer=brief_results.

Shen Congwen 沈从文 (1902–1988)
Alisi Zhongguo youji 阿丽思中国游记, 1928, online text: http://www.dushu369.com/zhongguomingzhu/scwzpj/alszgyj/.

Ba jun tu 八骏图, 1935, online text: http://www.millionbook.com/mj/s/shencongwen/bjt/002.htm.
"Eight Steeds," trans. William MacDonald, in *Imperfect Paradise: Shen Congwen*, ed. Jeffrey C. Kinkley, U. of Hawai'i Press, 1995, 346–77.

Shengshi di taitai 绅士的太太, 1929, online text: http://www.bwsk.com/MJ/s/shencongwen/scwz/002.htm.

Shen Qifeng 沈起鳳 (1741–?)
Xie duo 諧鐸, 1791, online text: https://zh.m.wikisource.org/zh-hant/%E8%AB%A7%E9%90%B8.

Shen Rong 谌容 (1936–)

Jianqu shisui 减去十岁, 1986, Online text: https://www.kekeshici.com/xiaoshuo/mingpian/193486.html.
"Ten Years Deducted," trans. Gladys Yang, in *At Middle Age*, Panda Books, 1987, 343–64.

Lande lihun 懒得离婚, 1988: https://www.worldcat.org/title/lan-de-li-hun/oclc/1242236068&referer=brief_results.

Ren dao zhongnian 人到中年, 1980, online text: https://www.99csw.com/book/2683/index.htm.
"At Middle Age," trans. Yu Fanqin and Wang Mingjie, in *At Middle Age*, Panda Books, 1987, 9–85.
Taizi cun de mimi 太子村的秘密, 1983: https://www.worldcat.org/title/tai-zi-cun-de-mi-mi/oclc/13745824&referer=brief_results.
"The Secret of Crown Prince Village," trans. Gladys Yang, in *At Middle Age*, Panda Books, 1987, 237–342.

Zhenzhen jiajia 真真假假, 1982: https://www.worldcat.org/title/zhen-zhen-jia-jia/oclc/1242236243&referer=brief_results.
"Snakes and Ladders," trans. Geremie Barmé and Linda Jaivin, in *At Middle Age*, Panda Books, 1987, 119–236.

Shi Tuo 师陀 (1910–1988)

Shi Tuo quanji 师陀全集, 2004: https://www.worldcat.org/title/shi-tuo-quan-ji/oclc/1183324368&referer=brief_results.

Shu Xi 束皙 (ca. 261–300)

Quan nong fu 劝农赋, Western Jin, online text: https://zh.m.wikisource.org/zh-hans/%E5%8B%B8%E8%BE%B2%E8%B3%A6.
"Ch'üan-nung fu," trans. Lien-sheng Yang, in "Notes on the Economic History of the Chin Dynasty," *Harvard Journal of Asiatic Studies* 9.2, 1946, 134 (doesn't translate the last twenty-six characters from 《太平御览》卷六百五十刑法部十六补).

Song Zhidi 宋之的 (1914–1956)

Qun hou 羣猴, 1949: https://www.worldcat.org/title/qun-hou/oclc/645708201&referer=brief_results.

Wu Chongqing 雾重庆, 1940: https://www.worldcat.org/title/wu-chongqing-wu-mu-hua-ju/oclc/49894930&referer=brief_results.

Su Shi 苏轼 (1037–1101) (attrib.)

Aizi zashuo 艾子杂说, Song Dynasty, online text: https://www.zhonghuadiancang.com/xueshuzaji/aizizashuo/ (has both an unpunctuated and punc-tuated version).

Sui Jingchen 睢景臣 (ca. 1275–ca. 1320)

Shaobian·Gaozu huanxiang 哨遍·高祖还乡, Yuan Dynasty, online text: https://www.thn21.com/wen/show/36727.html.
"Tune: Whistling Around·The Emperor's Home-coming," trans. Xu Yuanchong, in *300 Yuan Songs = Yuanqu sanbai shou*, Haitun chubanshe, 2013, 82–85. (哨遍 is the first of eight tunes under 高祖还乡.)

Tang Tao 唐弢 (1913–1992)

Tang Tao zawen xuan 唐弢雜文選, 1955: https://www.worldcat.org/title/dang-tao-za-wen-xuan/oclc/122728649&referer=brief_results.

Tang Xianzu 汤显祖 (1550–1616)

Handan ji 邯郸记, Ming Dynasty, online text: http://www.cngdwx.com/yuanmingqing/handanji/.
邯郸记, 汪榕培英译, 徐朔方笺校 = *The Handan Dream*, trans. Wang Rongpei, annot. Xu Shuofang, 外语教学与研究出版社, 2003 (bilingual).

Tang Yin 唐寅 (1470–1524)

Xi mei fu 惜梅赋, Ming Dynasty, online text: https://baike.baidu.com/item/%E6%83%9C%E6%A2%85%E8%B5%8B/60276263?fr=aladdin.

Tao Yin (unknown)

An Anthology of Chinese Humour, Joint Pub., 1987 (by subject).

Tian Han 田汉 (1898–1968)

Liren xing: Ershiyi chang huaju 麗人行: 二十一場话剧, 1946–1947, online text: https://www.zhonghuadiancang.com/shicixiqu/12903/.

Tianranchisou 天然痴叟 (unknown)

Tanlan han liu yuan mai fengliu 贪婪汉六院卖风流, c. 1628, online text: https://ctext.org/wiki.pl?if=gb&chapter=651306&remap=gb (石点头, ch. 8).

Wang Chong 王充 (27–97?/post 100)

Ci Meng pian 刺孟篇, Han Dynasty, online text: http://www.guoxuemeng.com/guoxue/7569.html (論衡·卷十).
"Censures on Mencius," trans. Alfred Forke, in *Lun-hêng*, trans. and annot. Alfred Forke, O. Harrasowitz, 1907, pt. 1, 418–32. (This book is in the public domain, available at archive.org.)

Weng Kong pian 问孔篇, Han Dynasty, online text: http://www.guoxuemeng.com/guoxue/7567.html (論衡·卷九).
"Criticisms on Confucius," trans. Alfred Forke, in *Lun-hêng*, trans. and annot. Alfred Forke, O. Harrasowitz, 1907, pt. 1, 392–417. (This book is in the public domain, available at archive.org.)

Wang Fu 王敷 (unknown)

Cha jiu lun 茶酒论, Tang Dynasty, online text: https://baike.baidu.com/item/%E8%8C%B6%E9%85%92%E8%AE%BA/1297704.
"A Dialogue between Mr. Tea and Mr. Wine, in one roll, with preface," trans. Chen Tsu-lung, in *Sinologica*, 6.4, 1961, 277–84.

Wang Ganrong 王干荣 (unknown)

Ji yan guan shimao 畸眼观时髦, 2003: https://www.worldcat.org/title/ji-yan-guan-shi-mao-jiyan-guan-shimao/oclc/52945126&referer=brief_results.

Wang Heqing 王和卿 (unknown)

Zuizhongtian·Yong da hudie 醉中天·咏大蝴蝶, Yuan Dynasty, online text: https://www.jianshu.com/p/7f2aa44a96c2.
"Tune: A Drinker's Sky·Song of a Huge Butterfly," trans. Xu Yuanchong, in *300 Yuan Songs = Yuanqu sanbai shou*, Haitun chubanshe, 2013, 25.

Wang Jiusi 王九思 (1468–1551)

Gujiu youchun 沽酒遊春, Ming Dynasty: https://www.worldcat.org/title/gu-jiu-you-chun/oclc/1194820880&referer=brief_results.

"Wang Chiu-ssu: The Wolf of Chung-shan," trans. J. I. Crump, in *Renditions*, 7, 1977, 29–38.

Wang Meng 王蒙 (1934–)

Feng xi lang zhi 风息浪止, 1983, in 王蒙文存: https://www.worldcat.org/title/wang-meng-wen-cun/oclc/53973846&referer=brief_results, v. 9, 458–502.

Jianying de xizhou 坚硬的稀粥, 1989, online text: https://www.99csw.com/article/311.htm.
"The Stubborn Porridge," in *The Stubborn Porridge and Other Stories*, trans. Zhu Hong, George Braziller, 1994, 8–38.

Qing hu 青狐, 2004: https://www.worldcat.org/title/qing-hu/oclc/1006753596&referer=brief_results.

Wang Pan 王磐 (ca. 1470–1530)

Chaotianzi·Yong laba 朝天子·咏喇叭, Ming Dynasty, online text: https://www.thn21.com/wen/show/36357.html.

Wang Shiwei 王实味 (1906–1947)

Ye baihehua 野百合花, 1942, online text: https://www.zhonghuadiancang.com/wenxueyishu/yebaihehua/150703.html.
"Wild Lily," in *Wild Lily, Prairie Fire: China's Road to Democracy, Yan'an to Tian'anmen, 1942–1989*, ed. Gregor Benton and Alan Hunter, Princeton UP, 1995, 69–75.

Wang Shizhen 王世贞 (1526–1590)

Laofu fu 老妇赋, Ming Dynasty, online text:
https://baike.baidu.com/item/%E8%80%81%E5%A6%87%E8%B5%8B/22688047?fr=aladdin.

Wang Shuo 王朔 (1958–)

Qianwan bie ba wo dang ren 千万别把我当人, 1989, online text:
https://www.99csw.com/book/2436/index.htm.
Please Don't Call Me Human, trans. Howard Goldblatt, Hyperion East, 2000.

Wan de jiushi xintiao 玩的就是心跳, 1989, online text:
https://www.99csw.com/book/2432/index.htm.
Playing for Thrills, trans. Howard Goldblatt, W. Morrow, 1997.

Wan zhu 顽主, 1987, online text: https://www.99csw.com/book/2434/index.htm.

Xin kuangren riji 新狂人日记, 2016: https://www.worldcat.org/title/xin-kuang-ren-ri-ji/oclc/1159296238&referer=brief_results.

Wang Tingxiang 王廷相 (1474–1544)

Menghu fu bing xu 猛虎赋并序, Ming Dynasty, in 历代赋鉴赏辞典:
https://www.worldcat.org/title/li-dai-fu-jian-shang-ci-dian/oclc/1057707452&referer=brief_results, 884–86 (including annotations and appreciation).

Wang Tongzhao 王统照 (1897–1957)

Haosheng 号声, 1928, online text: https://read.lmeee.com/download/engnj5.

Shuang hen 霜痕, 1932, online text: https://m.bsmao.com/shuanghen/.

Yi ye 一叶, 1922, online text: https://www.zhonghuadiancang.com/wenxueyishu/yiye/.

Wang Zhenhe 王祯和 (1940–1990)

Jiazhuang yi niuche 嫁妆一牛车, 1967, online text:
https://www.now818.com/post/12100.html.
"An Oxcart for a Dowry," trans. the author and Jon Jackson, in *The Columbia Anthology of Modern Chinese Literature*, ed. Joseph S.M. Lau and Howard Goldblatt, Columbia UP, 1995, 255–76.

Meigui meigui wo ai ni 玫瑰玫瑰我爱你, 1984: https://www.worldcat.org/title/mei-gui-mei-gui-wo-ai-ni/oclc/31127718&referer=brief_results.

Xiaolin lai Taibei 小林來台北, 1975, in 嫁粧一牛車: https://www.worldcat.org/title/jia-zhuang-yi-niu-che/oclc/18123249&referer=brief_results, 219–48.

Wen Yiduo 闻一多 (1899–1946)

Sishui 死水, 1926, online text: http://www.dushu369.com/shici/HTML/69706.html. "Stagnant Water," in *Stagnant Water: & Other Poems*, trans. Robert Hammond Dorsett, Brightcity, 2014, 27.

Wu Cheng'en 吴承恩 (ca. 1500–ca. 1582)

Xiyou Ji 西游记, 1560, online text: http://www.dushu369.com/gudianmingzhu/xyj/. *The Journey to the West*, rev. ed., trans. and ed. Anthony C. Yu, U. of Chicago Press, 2012, 4 vols.

Wu Jianren 吴趼人 (1866–1910)

Qiaopihua 俏皮话, 卢叔度辑注, 1981: https://www.worldcat.org/title/qiao-pi-hua/oclc/708717895&referer=brief_results.

Wofoshanren huaji tan 我佛山人滑稽谈, 1915: https://www.worldcat.org/title/wofoshanren-hua-ji-tan/oclc/936401389&referer=brief_results.

Xin Shitou ji 新石頭記, 1908, online text: https://www.shutxt.com/gudai/10108/.

Wu Kuan 吴寬 (1435–1504)

Ai liumin ci 哀流民辞, Ming Dynasty, in *Jia cang ji* 家藏集: https://www.worldcat.org/title/jia-cang-ji-77-juan-bu-yi-1-juan/oclc/221530130&referer=brief_results, 卷 57.

Wu Zuguang 吴祖光 (1917–2003)

Zhuo gui zhuan 捉鬼傳, 1947: https://www.worldcat.org/title/zhuo-gui-zhuan/oclc/679658329&referer=brief_results.

Wu Zuxiang 吴组缃 (1908–1994)

Fan yu ji 飯餘集, 1936: https://www.worldcat.org/title/fan-yu-ji/oclc/370584137&referer=brief_results.

Taishan fengguang 泰山风光, 1935, online text: http://www.dushu369.com/shici/HTML/31592.html.

Xi liu ji 西柳集, 1934: https://www.worldcat.org/title/xi-liu-ji/oclc/148110031&referer=brief_results.

Xia Yan 夏衍 (1900–1995)

Sai Jinhua 赛金花, 1936: https://www.worldcat.org/title/saijinhua-li-shi-ming-ju/oclc/885218912&referer=brief_results.

Xiao Hong 萧红 (1911–1942)

Ma Bole 马伯乐, 1981, online text: https://m.qidian.com/book/1019490453.html.

Xiao Yingshi 萧颖士 **(717–768)**

Fa yingtao shu fu 伐樱桃树赋, Tang Dynasty, online text: https://www.zhonghuadiancang.com/leishuwenji/13446/265926.html (scroll down, unpunctuated).

Xiong Foxi 熊佛西 **(1900–1965)**

Yang zhuangyuan 洋状元, 1927, in 佛西戲劇 第1集: https://www.worldcat.org/title/foxi-xi-ju-di-1-ji/oclc/28450663&referer=brief_results.

Xizhou Sheng 西周生 **(unknown) (in dispute)**

Xing shi yinyuan zhuan 醒世姻缘传, late Ming early Qing, online text: http://www.dushu369.com/gudianmingzhu/xsyyz/.

Xu Dishan 许地山 **(1893–1941)**

Xu Dishan zuopin ji 许地山作品集, 2018, online text: http://www.dushu369.com/zhongguomingzhu/xdsjpj/.

Xu Fuguan 徐復觀 **(1903–1982)**

Xu Fuguan zawen 徐復觀雜文, 1980: https://www.worldcat.org/title/xu-fu-guan-za-wen/oclc/815621860&referer=brief_results, 4 vols.

Xu Kun 徐坤 **(1965–)**

Rego 热狗, 2015: https://www.worldcat.org/title/re-gou/oclc/914289664&referer=brief_results.

Xianfeng 先锋, 1995: https://www.worldcat.org/title/xian-feng/oclc/34584231&referer=brief_results.

Zaoyu aiqing 遭遇爱情, 2017: https://www.worldcat.org/title/zao-yu-ai-qing/oclc/988754399&referer=brief_results (title story).

Xu Wei 徐渭 **(1521–1593)**

Ge dai xiao 歌代啸, Ming Dynasty, online text: https://zh.m.wikisource.org/zh-hans/%E6%AD%8C%E4%BB%A3%E5%95%B8.

Xu Xianzhong 徐献忠 **(1469–1545)**

Bu fu bing xu 布赋并序, Ming Dynasty, in 历代赋鉴赏辞典: https://www.worldcat.org/title/li-dai-fu-jian-shang-ci-dian/oclc/1057707452&referer=brief_results, 902–09 (including annotations and appreciation).

Xu Xiaobin 徐小斌 **(1953–)**

Lianyu zhi hua 炼狱之花, 2010: https://www.worldcat.org/title/lian-yu-zhi-hua-xin-ban/oclc/1243213951&referer=brief_results.

Xu Zhenqing 徐祯卿 (1479–1511)

Chou nü fu 丑女赋, Ming Dynasty, online text:
https://baike.baidu.com/item/%E4%B8%91%E5%A5%B3%E8%B5%8B/23148886?fr=aladdin.

Xuan Yongguang 宣永光 (1886–1960)

Fenghua jicheng 疯话集成, 1997: https://www.worldcat.org/title/feng-hua-ji-cheng/oclc/41037648&referer=brief_results.

Wang tan, fenghua 妄谈. 疯话, 1996: https://www.worldcat.org/title/wang-tan-feng-hua/oclc/36319507&referer=brief_results.

Yan Lianke 阎连科 (1958–)

Ding zhuang meng 丁庄梦, 2006: https://www.worldcat.org/title/ding-zhuang-meng/oclc/1235844083&referer=brief_results.
Dream of Ding Village, trans. Cindy Carter, Grove, 2009.

Fengya song 风雅颂, 2008, online text: https://www.sto.cx/book-28341-1.html.

Jianying ru shui 坚硬如水, 2001, online text:
https://www.99csw.com/book/2333/index.htm.
Hard like Water, trans. Carlos Rojas, Grove, 2021.

Ri xi 日熄, 2015: https://www.worldcat.org/title/ri-xi/oclc/1235838562&referer=brief_results.
The Day the Sun Died: A Novel, trans. Carlos Rojas, Grove, 2018.

Shou huo 受活, 2004, online text: https://www.shutxt.com/mz/8345/.
Lenin's Kisses, trans. Carlos Rojas, Grove, 2012.

Sishu 四書, 2010: https://www.worldcat.org/oclc/1227022937&referer=brief_results.
The Four Books, trans. Carlos Rojas, Grove, 2015.

Zhalie zhi 炸裂志, 2013, online text: https://m.shutxt.com/xiandai/19379/.
The Explosion Chronicles, trans. Carlos Rojas, Grove, 2016.

Yan Lieshan 鄢烈山 (1952–) (文)

Diandeng de quanli 点灯的权利, 2011: https://www.worldcat.org/title/dian-deng-de-quan-li/oclc/862759358?referer=di&ht=edition.

Yi ge ren de jingdian 一個人的经典, 周喜悦图, 2003:
https://www.worldcat.org/oclc/1293263996&referer=brief_results.

Yang Chaoguan 杨潮观 (1710–1788)

Yin feng ge zaju 吟風閣雜劇, Qing Dynasty: https://www.worldcat.org/title/yin-feng-ge-za-ju/oclc/802250314&referer=brief_results.

Yang Gu 陽固 (467–523)

Ci chan ji bi xing shi 刺谗疾嬖幸诗, Northern Wei, in 北史卷四十七 列传第三十五, under 阳尼传, online text: http://www.dushu369.com/gudianmingzhu/HTML/3376.html (scroll down). (For a *baihua* translation of the appended biography of Yang Gu under 阳尼传, see https://www.zhonghuadiancang.com/lishizhuanji/9020/178536.html, which leaves the last three punctuated sentences untranslated.)

Yang Hansheng 阳翰笙 (1902–1993)

Liangmian ren 两面人, 1943: https://www.worldcat.org/title/liang-mian-ren-you-ming-tian-di-xuan-huang-si-mu-xi-ju/oclc/40919202&referer=brief_results.

Yang Jiang 楊絳 (1911–2016)

Chenxinruyi 稱心如意, 1947: https://www.worldcat.org/title/cheng-xin-ru-yi-si-mu-xi-ju/oclc/59822474&referer=brief_results.

Feng xu 風絮, 1947: https://www.worldcat.org/title/feng-xu/oclc/20250666&referer=brief_results.

Nong zhen cheng jia 弄真成假, 1945: https://www.worldcat.org/title/nong-zhen-cheng-jia-wu-mu-xi-ju/oclc/1099274820&referer=brief_results.

Yang Kui 楊逵 (1905–1985)

Yang Kui xuanji 楊逵選集, 叢甦選, 1986: https://www.worldcat.org/title/yang-kui-xuan-ji/oclc/988679990&referer=brief_results.

Yang Shen 杨慎 (1488–1559)

Hou wen fu 后蚊赋, Ming Dynasty, online text: https://zh.m.wikisource.org/zh-hans/%E6%AC%BD%E5%AE%9A%E5%8F%A4%E4%BB%8A%E5%9C%96%E6%9B%B8%E9%9B%86%E6%88%90/%E5%8D%9A%E7%89%A9%E5%BD%99%E7%B7%A8/%E7%A6%BD%E8%9F%B2%E5%85%B8/%E7%AC%AC173%E5%8D%B7 (scroll down).

Wen fu 蚊赋, Ming Dynasty, online text: https://zh.m.wikisource.org/zh-hans/%E6%AC%BD%E5%AE%9A%E5%8F%A4%E4%BB%8A%E5%9C%96%E6%9B%B8%E9%9B%86%E6%88%90/%E5%8D%9A%E7%89%A9%E5%BD%99%E7%B7%A8/%E7%A6%BD%E8%9F%B2%E5%85%B8/%E7%AC%AC173%E5%8D%B7 (scroll down, the 2nd 蚊赋).

Yang Xiong 扬雄 (53 B.C.–18 A.D.)

Jiechao 解嘲, Western Han, online text:
https://www.zhonghuadiancang.com/shicixiqu/13575/.
"Dissolving Ridicule," trans. David R. Knechtges, in *The Han Rhapsody: A Study of the* Fu *of Yang Hsiung (53 B.C.–A.D. 18)*, Cambridge UP, 97–103.

Yang Xuewu 杨学武

Wenren de zhengzhi youzhibing: Yang Xuewu zawen zixuan ji 文人的政治幼稚病: 杨学武杂文自选集, 2016: https://www.worldcat.org/title/wen-ren-de-zheng-zhi-you-zhi-bing-yang-xuewu-za-wen-zi-xuan-ji/oclc/961185940&referer=brief_results.

For more titles in the series, 中国当代杂文精品大系, see
https://www.worldcat.org/search?qt=hotseries&q=se%3A%22Zhongguo+dang+dai+za+wen+jing+pin+da+xi%2C1949-2013%22.

Yang Zhifa 杨志发 (unknown) (编)

Zhongguo gujin xiehouyu daquan 中国古今歇后语大全, 2010:
https://www.worldcat.org/title/zhong-guo-gu-jin-xie-hou-yu-da-quan/oclc/880228341&referer=brief_results.

Yanxiasanren/Liu Zhang 烟霞散人/刘璋 (1667–?)

Zhan gui zhuan 斩鬼转, 1688, online text:
https://www.zhonghuadiancang.com/wenxueyishu/zhanguizhuan/.

Ye Shengtao 叶圣陶 (1894–1988)

Gemo 隔膜, 1922: https://www.worldcat.org/title/ge-mo/oclc/1266140721&referer=brief_results.

Huangdi de xin yi 皇帝的新衣, 1930, online text:
http://www.dushu369.com/tonghua/HTML/97772.html.

Huozai 火灾, 1923: https://www.worldcat.org/title/huo-zai/oclc/645936130&referer=brief_results.

Xian xia 线下, 1925: https://www.worldcat.org/title/xian-xia/oclc/862707394&referer=brief_results.

Ye Zhaoyan 叶兆言 (1957–)

Wuyue de huanghun 五月的黄昏, 2001: https://www.worldcat.org/title/wu-yue-de-huang-hun/oclc/646350337&referer=brief_results.

Zaoshu de gushi 枣树的故事, online text: https://www.kanunu8.com/book4/8735/.

Youxizhuren 遊戲主人 (unknown)

Xiaolin guang ji 笑林廣記, Qing Dynasty, online text: https://www.haoshuya.com/9/6457/.

笑林广记选: 汉英对照插图本 = *A Collection of Classic Chinese Jokes*, 郑孝先, 袁孝竞 选译, 外文出版社, 2011 (bilingual selections).

Yu Hua 余华 (1960–)

Xianshi yi zhong 现实一种, 1988, online text: https://www.99csw.com/book/2421/index.htm.

"One Kind of Reality," trans. Jeanne Tai, in *Running Wild: New Chinese Writers*, ed. David Der-wei Wang with Jeanne Tai, Columbia UP, 1994, 21–68.

Xiongdi 兄弟, 2005, online text: https://www.mengruan.com/xiongdi/.
Brothers, trans. Eileen Cheng-yin Chow and Carlos Rojas, Pantheon, 2009.

Yijiubaliu nian 一九八六年, 2013: https://www.worldcat.org/oclc/1302227031&referer=brief_results.

Yuan Muzhi 袁牧之 (1909–1978)

Yi ge nüren he yi tiao gou 一个女人和一条狗, c. 1928–1929, in 袁牧之全集: https://www.worldcat.org/title/yuan-muzhi-quan-ji/oclc/1152146326&referer=brief_results, v. 2.

Yuan Shuipai 袁水拍 (1916–1982)

Ma Fantuo di shange (1944–1948) (*xuan*) 马凡陀的山歌 (1944–1948) (选), online text: https://www.marxists.org/chinese/reference-books/poems-of-struggle/china-mafantuo.htm (9 pieces), full version: https://www.worldcat.org/title/ma-fantuo-di-shan-ge/oclc/35553231&referer=brief_results.

Ma Fantuo di shange: Xuji 馬凡陀的山歌: 續集, 1978?: https://www.worldcat.org/title/ma-fantuo-de-shan-ge-xu-ji/oclc/35561156&referer=brief_results.

Soy Sauce and Prawns: Satiric Political Verse, trans. Sydney Shapiro, Foreign Languages Press, 1963.

Zhengzhi fengci shi 政治讽刺诗, 1966: https://www.worldcat.org/title/zheng-zhi-feng-ci-shi/oclc/1101312250?referer=di&ht=edition.

Yuan Zhen 元稹 (779–831)

Tang Song chuanqi 唐宋传奇, 元稹等著, Tang Dynasty: https://www.worldcat.org/title/tang-song-chuan-qi/oclc/953271165&referer=brief_results, *Selected Chinese Short Stories of the Tang and Song Dynasties*, trans. Yang Xianyi, Gladys Yang, Huang Jun, Foreign Language[s] Press, 2001 (21 stories).

Yuefu 樂府, Tang Dynasty, in *Yuan Zhen ji* 元稹集: https://www.worldcat.org/oclc/1280950123&referer=brief_results, v. 1, 254–312.

Yunzhongdaoren 雲中道人 (unknown)

Tang Zhong Kui ping gui zhuan 唐钟馗平鬼传, 1785, online text: https://www.dushu.com/showbook/100723/.

Zang Kejia 臧克家 (1905–2004)

Baobei er 寶貝兒, 1946: https://www.worldcat.org/title/bao-bei-er/oclc/680449457&referer=brief_results.

Shengming de lingdu 生命的零度, 1947: https://www.worldcat.org/title/sheng-ming-ti-ling-tu/oclc/951018365&referer=brief_results.
Zang Kejia shi xuan 臧克家诗选, 1956: https://www.worldcat.org/title/zang-ke-jia-shi-xuan/oclc/1265968219&referer=brief_results.

Zeng Pu 曾朴 (1872–1935)

Nie hai hua 孽海花, 1941, online text: http://www.dushu369.com/gudianmingzhu/nhh/.
A Flower in a Sinful Sea, trans. Rafe de Crespigny and Liu Ts'un-yan, *Renditions*, nos. 17 & 18, 1982, 137–92, online pdf: https://www.cuhk.edu.hk/rct/pdf/e_outputs/b1718/v17&18P137.pdf (1st 5 chapters).

Zhang Dachun 张大春 (1957–)

Da shuohuang jia 大说谎家, 1989: https://www.worldcat.org/title/da-shuo-huang-jia/oclc/32523771&referer=brief_results.

Mei ren xiexin gei shangxiao 沒人寫信給上校, 1994: https://www.worldcat.org/title/mei-ren-xie-xin-gei-shang-xiao/oclc/1256513717&referer=brief_results.

Zhang Guodong 张国动 (unknown) (主编)

Zhongguo lidai fengci shi xuan zhu 中国历代讽刺诗选注, 2012: https://www.worldcat.org/oclc/1301762424&referer=brief_results.

Zhang Heng 张衡 (78–139)

Xijing fu 西京赋, Eastern Han, online text: https://baike.baidu.com/item/%E8%A5%BF%E4%BA%AC%E8%B5%8B, "Western Metropolis Rhapsody," in Xiao Tong, *Wen xuan, or, Selections of Refined Literature*, trans. with annotations and intro. David R. Knechtges, Princeton UP, 1982, v. 1, 181–242.

Zhang Henshui 张恨水 (1895–1967)

Bashan ye yu 巴山夜雨, 1946, online text: https://www.99csw.com/book/4175/index.htm.

Bashiyi meng 八十一梦, 1939, online text: https://www.99csw.com/book/9849/index.htm.

Wangliang shijie 魍魉世界, 1941, online text: https://www.zhonghuadiancang.com/wenxueyishu/wangliangshijie/.

Zhi zui jin mi 纸醉金迷, 1946, online text: https://www.99csw.com/book/4174/index.htm.

Zhang Jie 张洁 (1937–2022)
As Long as Nothing Happens, Nothing Will, trans. Gladys Yang, Deborah J. Leonard, and Zhang Andong, Grove Weidenfeld, 1991 (contains 他有什么病?, 119–96).

Hong mogu 红蘑菇, 1991: https://www.worldcat.org/title/hong-mo-gu/oclc/953747640&referer=brief_results.

Love Must Not Be Forgotten, intro. Gladys Yang, trans. Gladys Yang, et al., China Books & Periodicals / Panda Books, 1986 (contains 条件尚未成熟, 63–77).

Shanghuo 上火, 1991, online text: https://www.99csw.com/book/10235/368961.htm.

Zhiyou yi ge taiyang 只有一个太阳, 1989, online text: https://www.99csw.com/book/10230/index.htm.

Zhang Kejiu 张可久 (ca. 1270–ca. 1350)
Zuitaiping·Ren jie xian ming jiong 醉太平·人皆嫌命窘, Yuan Dynasty, online text: https://baike.baidu.com/item/%E9%86%89%E5%A4%AA%E5%B9%B3%C2%B7%E4%BA%BA%E7%9A%86%E5%AB%8C%E5%91%BD%E7%AA%98.

Zhang Mingshan 张鸣善 (unknown)
Shuixianzi·Ji shi 水仙子·讥时, Yuan Dynasty, online text: https://baike.baidu.com/item/%E6%B0%B4%E4%BB%99%E5%AD%90%C2%B7%E8%AE%A5%E6%97%B6/4075463.

Zhang Nanzhuang 张南庄 (unknown)
He dian 何典, 1879, online text: https://www.99csw.com/book/590/index.htm.

Zhang Tianyi 张天翼 (1906–1985)
Baoshi fuzi 包氏父子, 1934, online text: http://www.dushu369.com/qtyd/bsfz/.

Gui tu riji 鬼土日记, 1931, online text : https://www.zhonghuadiancang.com/wenxueyishu/13079/.

Hua Wei xiansheng 华威先生, 1938, online text:
http://www.dushu369.com/shici/HTML/62255.html.
Mr. Huawei=Huawei xiansheng, trans. Charles A. Liu, Chaire L. Scarano, Princeton U., 1976?.

Jin ya diguo 金鸭帝国, written before 1949:
https://www.worldcat.org/title/jin-ya-di-guo/oclc/898226762&referer=brief_results.

Zhang Tianyi fengci xiaoshuo 张天翼讽刺小说, 张大明编, 2018:
https://www.worldcat.org/title/zhang-tian-yi-feng-ci-xiao-shuo/oclc/1097985257&referer=brief_results.

Zhang Xianliang 张贤亮 (1936–2014)
Langman de hei pao 浪漫的黑炮, 1984, online text:
http://www.dushu369.com/zhongguomingzhu/zxlwj/lmdhp/.

Wo de puti shu 我的菩提树, 1994: https://www.worldcat.org/title/wo-de-pu-ti-shu/oclc/910714981&referer=brief_results.
My Bodhi Tree, trans. Martha Avery, Secker & Warburg, 1996.

Zhang Xiguo 張系國 (1944–)
Youzi hun zuqu 遊子魂組曲, 1989: https://www.worldcat.org/title/you-zi-hun-zu-qu/oclc/21189761&referer=brief_results

Zhang Xinxin 张辛欣 (1953–)
Fengkuang de junzilan 疯狂的君子兰, 1983, in 张辛欣小说集:
https://www.worldcat.org/title/zhang-xinxin-xiao-shuo-ji/oclc/23240034&referer=brief_results, 304–26.
"Mad about Orchids," trans. Helen Wang, 2011: https://www.academia.edu/5983073.

Zhao Yi 赵壹 (ca. 130–ca. 185, alt. ca. 153–212)
Ci shi ji xie fu 刺世疾邪赋, Eastern Han, online text:
https://baike.baidu.com/item/%E5%88%BA%E4%B8%96%E7%96%BE%E9%82%AA%E8%B5%8B/9497769.
"*Fù* Satirizing the Age, Detesting Iniquity," in *A Significant Season: Cai Yong (ca. 133–192) and His Contemporaries*, Mark Laurent Asselin, American Oriental Society, 2010, 329–37.

Zhao Yi 趙翼 (1727–1814)
Oubei ji 甌北集, Qing Dynasty: https://www.worldcat.org/title/oubei-ji/oclc/170894767&referer=brief_results, 2 vols.

Zheng Tingyu 郑廷玉 (active 1251)
Kan qian nu mai yuanjia zhaizhu, 看钱奴买冤家债主, Yuan Dynasty, online text:
http://www.dushu369.com/gudianmingzhu/HTML/22180.html.

Zhongguo tanguan shujuku 中国贪官数据库

Honglou yi meng heshi xing, xiyou guohou zai fengshen, shuihu yibai ling ba meng, xixiang xian ju hou sanguo 红楼一梦何时醒, 西游过后再封神, 水浒壹佰零捌蒙, 西厢先聚后三國, 2013, online text: https://tanguan.io/docs11/post/11/o4cgn2om/.

Zhou Wen 周文 (1907–1952)

Zhou Wen wenji 周文文集, 2011: https://www.worldcat.org/title/zhou-wen-wen-ji/oclc/1183071712&referer=brief_results, 4 vols.

Zhu Wen 朱文 (1967–)

The Matchmaker, the Apprentice, and the Football Fan: More Stories of China, trans. Julia Lovell, Columbia UP, 2013.

Zhuoyuantingzhuren 酌元亭主人 (active 17th c.)

Zhao shi bei 照世杯, c. 1661, online text: https://www.zhonghuadiancang.com/wenxueyishu/zhaoshibei/.

Zong Mi 宗密 (780–841)

Yuan ren lun 原人论, Tang Dynasty, online text: https://baike.baidu.com/item/%E5%8E%9F%E4%BA%BA%E8%AE%BA/6933353.

Made in the USA
Monee, IL
30 January 2025

02e20f2c-04c5-49cb-aa59-cd71438c4792R01